**IT IS YOUR WORLD AND
I APPRECIATE YOU
ALLOWING ME TO BE A
PART OF IT!**

**WITH LOVE AND
AFFECTION ALWAYS,**

TABLE OF CONTENTS

THE HILLS THAT ARE DREADED BY THOSE WHO TAKE SMALL STEPS

BY JOHN A. BOLDEN

JUDGEMENT DAY

ANCIENT WISDOM ABOUT TO UNFOLD
WORLD IN CHAOS SOULS ARE SOLD
THE DARK IS LIGHT AND LIGHT IS DARK
HEAVEN'S ANGELS WINGS EMBARK
THEY FEAST UPON THE HUMAN RAGE
BROUGHT ON BY GREED THIS UGLY PLAQUE
THEIR OWN FAULT NOW THIS IS TRUE
WITH HANDS THAT CLUTCH THEIR GREED LIKE GLUE
NEVER LEARNING
ALWAYS YEARNING
NEVER TEACHING
WHAT SHOULD BE TAUGHT
THEIR SELFISH WAYS IS TYRANNY WROUGHT
PROGRESS THROUGH LIFE THE LORD HAS SAID
MY GIFT TO YOU IS THE LIGHT YOU SHED
KNOWLEDGE BRINGS FORTH THE BETTER IN YOU
LEARN IT NOW AND TEACH IT TRUE
WHEN YOU HAVE PASSED AND YOUTH LIVES ON
YOUR SOUL SHALL GLIDE ON HEAVENS SONG!

WHEN I FIRST WROTE THAT POEM IN JANUARY OF 2004,
I THOUGHT TO MYSELF, "OH WOW, THAT SOUNDS
REALLY GOOD, I'VE GOT TO KEEP THAT". IT TOOK ME
ABOUT AN HOUR TO CREATE IT, NOT VERY LONG. AT
THE MOMENT, I REALLY DID NOT KNOW WHAT IT TRULY
DEFINED, SOUNDED GOOD AT THE TIME OF MY LIFE
WHEN MY WORLD SEEMED GLOOMY WITH NO HOPE.
BELIEVING IN SOMETHING, BUT NOT KNOWING WHAT,
BELIEVING IN GOD, BUT WITH LITTLE FAITH. CRYING

OUT WITH A LOUD VOICE, EVERY DAY AS I DROVE MY BIG RIG DOWN THE ROAD, "WHY ME?, WHY DOES EVERYTHING BAD HAPPEN TO ME IN MY LIFE?" SCREAMING AT THE TOP OF MY LUNGS, IN A HOUSE BY MYSELF, "WHAT IS IT THAT I HAVE TO DO TO MAKE MY LIFE RIGHT, IS THERE ANY HOPE FOR ME?" ANGRY AT A GOD WHOM I THOUGHT PLACED ME IN THAT POSITION, ANGRY AT MYSELF FOR HAVING PUT MYSELF IN THAT POSITION AND NOT DOING ANYTHING TO GET MYSELF OUT OF THAT, OR AT LEAST I THOUGHT I WASN'T AT THAT TIME. KNOWING WHAT I KNOW NOW, YES, GOD DID PUT ME IN THAT POSITION, AND YES, I ALSO PLACED MYSELF INTO THAT POSITION. I AM THE CREATOR AND THE CREATED OF MY WORLD AND GOD GIVES US EVERYTHING WE ASK FOR AND I AM VERY APPRECIATIVE FOR GOD'S GRACE TO GRANT US THIS. THE POEM, AS I KNOW NOW, WAS MY JUDGEMENT DAY. THIS WAS GOD'S WAY OF LETTING ME KNOW THAT HELP WAS, AND IS ALWAYS, ON THE WAY. AT THE TIME, I WAS HEARING AND WRITING DOWN THE WORDS BUT NOT LISTENING TO THEM OR THE MESSAGE IT CONVEYED. ANCIENT WISDOM HAS UNFOLDED BEFORE ME, MY WORLD WAS IN CHAOS, MY DARKNESS WAS THE TRUTH OF LIGHT TO BE EXPERIENCED, HEAVEN'S ANGELS WINGS HAVE EMBARKED UPON ME WITH THEIR MESSAGES AND I HAVE LISTENED, HEAVEN'S ANGELS FEAST UPON THE HUMAN RAGE OF CRYING OUT FOR HELP, FOR THEY ARE SO WILLING TO GIVE OF THIS GRACIOUSNESS TO THOSE WHO HAVE GREED IN THEIR HEARTS AND A DESIRE TO LOVE. GOD'S MESSENGERS ARE ALWAYS WILLING TO TEACH IF WE ARE WILLING TO REMEMBER, FOR ONCE WE REMEMBER "WHO WE REALLY ARE" WE CAN TEACH TO THOSE WHO ARE READY TO LISTEN AND TO

"RE-MEMBER"

THEMSELF. THEN WE CAN SHED THE LIGHT OF
KNOWLEDGE WITH OTHERS SO THAT OUR SOUL MAY
GLIDE UPON HEAVEN'S SONG. AS YOU SIT THEIR AND
READ THIS BOOK, KNOW NOW, THAT TODAY IS YOUR
JUDGEMENT DAY. YOU HAVE ASKED FOR THIS
KNOWLEDGE YOU ARE ABOUT TO READ,"ASK AND YE
SHALL RECEIVE". THIS IS NOT A COINCIDENCE THAT
YOU HAVE THIS BOOK IN HAND. THIS IS THE ANSWER TO
YOUR QUESTIONS THAT YOU HAVE ASKED. GOD HAS
GIVEN TO ME, THROUGH ME, TO GIVE TO YOU THIS
LIGHT OF KNOWLEDGE TO BE SHARED AMONG ALL OF
US.

THE WORDS YOU ARE ABOUT TO READ WILL COME TO
YOU LIKE A BRIGHT LIGHT BULB COMING DOWN FROM
THE HEAVENS AND IS IN FACT IS WHERE THIS
AWARENESS IS COMING FROM. MUCH OF WHAT YOU
WILL BE READING IS A COMPILATION OF DIFFERENT
AUTHORS AND SPEAKERS WHOSE WORDS OF WISDOM
ARE SHARED WITH YOU THROUGH THIS EXPRESSION.
FOR THEIR COURAGE AND STRENGTH TO BRING FORTH
SUCH ENLIGHTENMENT, I WISH TO APPRECIATE EACH
AND EVERYONE OF THEM. FOR THEY ARE TRULY
MESSENGERS OF GOD. NEALE DONALD WALSCH FOR
"CONVERSATION WITH GOD", JAMES REDFIELD "THE
CELESTINE PROPHECY", GREG BRADEN "THE GOD
CODE", DANNION BRINKLEY "YOU ARE A HIGHLY
POWERFUL SPIRITUAL BEING", DONNA FOX "THE
AKASHIC RECORDS", AND MANY OTHERS THAT ARE
PAST, PRESENT, AND FUTURE IN WHICH WE ALL LIVE IN
THE TIME FRAME OF "NOW". I DEDICATE THIS NEXT
POEM TO EACH AND EVERYONE OF US.

A SPIRIT OF GOD

FOR MANY IT STILL BOGGLES THEIR MIND

TO CONSIDER THEMSELVES EQUAL TO A GOD, SO KIND

FOR TO SPEAK GOD'S WORDS OF OPENNESS

IS TO BE SHAMED BY THOSE WITH UNHAPPINESS

THE LIGHT OF THE WORD SCARES THE LIFE OUT OF
MANY

FOR THEY DENY TO THEMSELVES A WORLD THAT IS
PLENTY

IT IS COURAGE AND STRENGTH TO BE A MESSENGER OF
GOD

FOR IT MEANS TO BE BURIED BENEATH THE COLD LADEN
SOD

THE RIDICULE

THE PAIN

THE EMBARRASSING SHAME

IS THE REWARD RECEIVED FOR SHARING GOD'S NAME

FOR THOSE WHO SEEK AND ACKNOWLEDGE THE LIGHT

BURST FORTH AND SHARE THEIR HEAVEN'S DELIGHT

THEY KNOW WHAT THEY KNOW AND WISH TO SHARE IT
WITH YOU

ACCEPT WHO YOU ARE AND BELIEVE IT SO TRUE

GIVE LOVE TO THOSE WHO HAVE OPENED THEIR HEART

PARTAKE OF THEIR GOODNESS, FOR THAT'S WHERE TO
START

THEY HAVE SOUGHT FOR THEIR WISDOM, FORTUNE, AND
FAME

HAVING FOUND ALL THE ANSWERS, THEY GIVE YOU THE

SAME

THEN GIVE TO THEM THE RESPECT THEY DESERVE

FOR IT IS IN GOD'S NAME THEY ACTUALLY SERVE

THEY SEEK NOT TO TAKE WHAT YOU THINK THAT YOU
OWN

FOR IN GOD'S KINGDOM THEY HAVE THEIR OWN THRONE

THEY KNOW THERE IS PLENTY, AN ABUNDANCE FOR ALL

THEY THINK IT, THEN SPEAK IT, THEN EXPERIENCE
THEIR CALL

THIS IS WHAT THEY TEACH, IF YOU LISTEN AND HEAR

ALL THAT THEY ASK IS THAT YOU LEND THEM YOUR EAR

IF YOU LISTEN AND KNOW

THE WORDS THEY DO SAY

A NEW WORLD SHALL OPEN AND START A NEW DAY

THE CLOUDS SHALL LIFT AND THE SUN WILL APPEAR

A WARMTH IN YOUR HEART AS LOVE SHALL DRAW NEAR

IT IS THIS THAT THEY SEEK FROM THE UNWILLING
MIND

FOR YOU TO KNOW YOUR EXISTENCE AND CEASE BEING
SO BLIND

WHEN YOU REACH THAT STEP

SO HIGH IN LIFE

AND CROSS THAT UNSEEN LINE

A SPIRIT OF GOD

SHALL FOREVER BE

ETERNAL

THROUGHOUT TIME!

JOHN A. BOLDEN

AUGUST 22, 2004

CREATION

EACH AND EVERYONE OF US CREATE OUR WORLD EVERY SECOND, EVERY MINUTE OF EVERY HOUR OF EVERY DAY. IF YOU DON'T THINK THAT YOU DO, THEN THINK AGAIN. IT IS DECLARING OWNERSHIP OF THIS CREATION THAT HAS MANY PEOPLE IN AN UPHEAVAL OF THEIR LIFE. YOU ARE UNCONSCIOUSLY CREATING A WORLD YOU ARE CONSCIOUSLY REACTING TO. WHAT YOU ARE ABOUT TO LEARN IS HOW TO CONSCIOUSLY CREATE YOUR WORLD SO THAT YOU MAY KNOW OF AND ENJOY YOUR CREATION. REMEMBER THIS AS YOU READ FURTHER, "THERE IS NOTHING RIGHT NOR WRONG, THERE IS NOTHING GOOD NOR BAD, THERE IS ONLY EXPERIENCE". IF SOMETHING YOU HAVE CREATED SERVES YOUR PURPOSE THEN KEEP IT WITH YOU, IN OTHER WORDS KEEP RECREATING IT, IF IT NO LONGER SERVES YOU, THEN THANK IT FOR THE EXPERIENCE, BLESS IT AND SEND IT BACK OUT INTO THE UNIVERSE. THE WHOLE PURPOSE OF LIFE IS TO EXPERIENCE WHATEVER WE WISH, AND LEAD US THROUGH OUR SPIRITUAL EVOLUTION OF BEING AS ONE WITH GOD. KNOWING OF OUR CREATION ABILITIES BRINGS US CLOSER TO THE ONENESS OF GOD. LET'S BEGIN OUR JOURNEY.

THOUGHTS OR THINKING
FIRST LEVEL OF CREATION

AS HUMAN BEINGS WE HAVE THOUGHTS. THOUGHTS ARE THE ENERGY OF THE SOUL, THE LANGUAGE OF OUR SOUL, THOUGHTS ARE OUR SOUL. MANY PEOPLE BELIEVE THE SOUL IS RETAINED INSIDE THE BODY, IN ALL ACTUALITY, OUR SOUL IS THE ENERGY THAT SURROUNDS OUR BODY, THE HUMAN AURA. OUR BODY IS A TOOL THAT ENABLES US TO EXPERIENCE OUR THOUGHT FORMS. THE ACTIVITIES WE CREATE WITHIN OUR THOUGHTS, THE FEELINGS, EVERYTHING AND ANYTHING WE CAN THINK OF. WE DO NOT THINK WITH OUR BRAIN, WE THINK WITH OUR SOUL. THE BRAIN IS MERELY A RECEPTION PART OF OUR BODY THAT ENABLES US TO EXPERIENCE LIFE AS HUMAN BEINGS. IT HELPS THE SOUL IN DETERMINING WHAT REALLY SERVES US WITH OUR EXPERIENCES. THIS IS THE FIRST STEP OF CREATION. YOUR THOUGHT FORM, YOUR THINKING, YOUR VISUALIZATION OF A CERTAIN PLACE, OR THING, OR FEELING, OR ACTION, IS THE GROUND FLOOR OF CREATION. NOW THINKING ABOUT SOMETHING ISN'T GOING TO MAKE IT HAPPEN. THERE IS A BIT MORE TO THIS. THE NEXT STEP IS TO VERBALLY SPEAK OUT THESE THOUGHT FORMS.

SPEAKING
SECOND LEVEL OF CREATION

YOU MUST SPEAK OF THAT WHICH YOU WISH TO EXPERIENCE. NOT A WHISPER BUT PRONOUNCE IT, COMMAND IT OUT LOUD, OR IN A CASUAL CONVERSATIONAL VOICE. THIS IS A VERY IMPORTANT PART OF CREATION, IT SETS INTO MOTION THE MANIFESTATION OF CREATION, ANYTHING THAT YOU HAVE THOUGHT OF. EVEN IF IT WAS A THOUGHT YOU

HAD TEN YEARS AGO THAT YOU THOUGHT MAY HAVE SERVED YOU BACK THEN BUT NO LONGER WOULD SERVE YOU AT THE PRESENT, BUT NEVER SPOKE OF IT TEN YEARS AGO, AND NOW EXPRESS IT TO SOMEONE IN A CASUAL CONVERSATION, YOU ARE GOING TO EXPERIENCE THAT THOUGHT WHETHER YOU LIKE IT OR NOT. THE UNIVERSE GIVES YOU EVERYTHING YOU ASK FOR, THIS IS WHY YOU WILL BE APPRECIATIVE FOR EACH AND EVERYDAY OF YOUR LIFE. THIS IS HOW IT WORKS, THAT WHICH IS THOUGHT OF BUT NEVER SPOKEN OF WILL ONLY CREATE UPON THE FIRST LEVEL OF CREATION, WHICH IS THOUGHT. THAT WHICH IS SPOKEN OF BUT NEVER THOUGHT OF WILL ONLY CREATE UPON THE SECOND LEVEL OF CREATION, WHICH IS SPEECH. THERE IS A CERTAIN WAY TO ASK FOR THESE EXPERIENCES AS WELL. THE SPEECH PATTERNS MUST BE CAREFULLY MONITORED BY YOURSELF. IF YOU LISTEN TO WHAT YOU ACTUALLY SPEAK OF, YOU CAN PREDICT YOUR OWN FUTURE. NEVER NEED NOR WANT FOR ANYTHING, ALWAYS KNOW THAT YOU HAVE AND BY "WILL" YOU SHALL HAVE IT. WHEN YOU SAY "I NEED THIS" OR "I WANT THAT", THE UNIVERSE LOOKS DOWN UPON YOU AND SAYS, "WHY OF COURSE YOU DO." BEING THAT THE UNIVERSE GIVES TO YOU EVERYTHING YOU ASK FOR, IT GIVES YOU EXACTLY THAT, THE NEEDINESS AND WANTINGNESS OF THAT. YOU WILL NEVER REALLY ACTUALLY RECEIVE THE ITEM OR EXPERIENCE YOU WERE ASKING FOR ORIGINALLY, UNLESS YOU SPEAK THE PROPER WORDS. ALWAYS BEGIN YOUR SENTENCES WITH

"I AM",

"I WILL",

"I HAVE"

"I WISH"

"I HOPE"

"I DESIRE".

IT IS NOT A COMPLICATED TASK TO CHANGE ONES
SPEECH PATTERNS, AFTER YEARS OF SPEAKING, IT CAN,
AND THY WILL, BE DONE. AS YOU LISTEN TO OTHERS
SPEAK, MENTALLY CHANGE THEIR WORDING AROUND IN
YOUR OWN MIND, THIS WILL HELP TO TRAIN YOU IN
YOUR THOUGHTS AND SPEECH. IT REALLY DOES WORK!
IF YOU ARE FEELING A BIT DOWN ONE DAY, DECLARE "I
AM THE HAPPINESS OF MY LIFE". THINK THIS AND SAY IT
OUT LOUD. LOVE THAT FEELING OF DEPRESSION,{AND
BY LOVE, I AM DEFINING LOVE AS "BE THANKFUL" OF
DEPRESSION FOR IT WAS YOUR CREATION TO BEGIN
WITH AND LIKE ANY OTHER ENTITY IT SEEKS
ACCEPTANCE FROM IT'S CREATOR, THIS WILL BE
EXPLAINED LATER ON}. AFTER YOU SAY "I AM THE
HAPPINESS OF MY LIFE." YOUR MIND WILL COME BACK
AT YOU WITH THAT INNER VOICE SAYING
SARCASTICALLY, "YEAH RIGHT, WHATEVER", THIS IS
THE NEGATIVE PORTION OF YOU COMING BACK AND
SEEKING YOUR ACCEPTANCE OF IT'S CREATION.
NEGATIVITY IS IN EXISTENCE WITHIN YOU AND LIKE
ANYTHING ELSE THAT IS IN EXISTENCE, IT HAS A
DEFENSE MECHANISM TO KEEP ITSELF ALIVE WITHIN
YOU! COME BACK AT IT AGAIN, OUT LOUD, "I AM THE
HAPPINESS OF MY LIFE", "I AM THE CREATOR OF MY
WORLD". THIS AFFIRMATION IS A VERY POWERFUL
TOOL, ESPECIALLY "I AM". NOTICE WITHIN A FEW
HOURS, YOU WILL BE A MUCH BRIGHTER, LIGHTER

SPIRIT. HAPPINESS BEGINS TO SETTLE IN. IT'S NOT JUST A BETTER DAY, IT IS A BETTER DAY THAT YOU HAVE CREATED. YOU, WITH YOUR ALMIGHTY POWERFUL SPIRITUAL BEING, HAVE JUST CREATED, FOR YOURSELF, A MUCH GREATER VISION OF THE GRANDEST VERSION OF YOU! THE CLOUDS HAVE LIFTED TO START A NEW DAY, AND NOW IT IS TIME FOR YOU TO "APPRECIATE", THIS WONDERFUL HAPPY DAY YOU HAVE CREATED. THIS LEADS US INTO THE THIRD PORTION OF CREATION.

EXPERIENCE
THIRD LEVEL OF CREATION

ONCE YOU HAVE VISUALIZED WHAT IT IS THAT YOU DESIRE, AND NOW HAVE SPOKEN THE CORRECT WORDING OF DESIRE, THE NEXT STEP IS TO ACTUALLY EXPERIENCE YOUR MANIFESTATION. CLAIM IT {REALIZING IT}, OWN IT {FEELING IT, KNOWING YOU HAVE CREATED IT}, AND BE "THANKFUL" OR "APPRECIATIVE" OF IT, DEPENDING ON WHETHER IT SERVES YOU OR NOT. WHEN YOU SAY

"THANK YOU", YOU PAST THINK IT AND IT CAN LEAVE YOUR LIFE OR YOUR EXPERIENCE.

WHEN YOU SAY,

"I APPRECIATE IT", YOU ARE SAYING YOU WISH TO GIVE IT GREATER VALUE INTO YOUR LIFE SO THAT IT MAY STAY WITHIN YOUR LIFE OR EXPERIENCE.

IT IS ALL "UP" TO YOU AS TO WHAT SERVES YOU. THIS IS TRAINING YOU TO BE CONSCIOUSLY AWARE OF

CREATING YOUR LIFE. YOU ARE FINALLY REALIZING, YOU, ARE CREATING YOUR LIFE INSTEAD OF REACTING TO IT. NOTICE THE DIFFERENCE IN THE WORDS,

"CREATING"

 AND

"REACTING",

SAME LETTERS TO PRODUCE THE WORD BUT IN DIFFERENT PLACEMENT. WHEN YOU CREATE, YOU ARE "C'ING"

YOUR LIFE FOR YOURSELF. NOW IS THE TIME FOR YOU TO DECIDE IF THIS EXPERIENCE ACTUALLY SERVES YOU. GRAB THE ESSENCE OF IT, EXPERIENCE EVERY BEING OF IT'S MANIFESTATION. IF YOU ENJOY IT, THEN KEEP IT WITH YOU, KEEP RECREATING IT, AND "APPRECIATE IT", FOR HAVING IT AS YOUR CREATION. IF IT DOESN'T SERVE YOU, THEN "THANK IT" FOR IT'S BEING AND THE EXPERIENCE YOU RECEIVED FROM IT, AND SEND IT BACK OUT INTO THE UNIVERSE. DON'T IGNORE IT AND THINK IT WILL GO AWAY. "FOR WHAT YOU RESIST, SHALL PERSIST". SOMETHING THAT YOU REALIZE NO LONGER SERVES YOU FOR YOUR PURPOSE, WILL NOT JUST GO AWAY, UNLESS YOU CLAIM OWNERSHIP OF IT'S CREATION, BECAUSE, YOU, IN FACT, HAVE CREATED THE MANIFESTATION OF IT'S PRESENCE. ACCEPT THAT RESPONSIBILITY, CLAIM YOUR CREATIONS, THEN THANK THOSE ENTITIES FOR THAT EXPERIENCE, AND LOVE THEM FOR IT, THEN SEND IT BACK INTO THE UNIVERSE. AFTER DOING THIS, AND ONLY AFTER DOING THAT, IS WHEN YOU CAN CHANGE THINGS AND CREATE ANEW.

THE COMBINATION

NOW, LET'S TAKE A LOOK AT THE THREE TOOLS WE MUST BE AWARE OF AND REMEMBER TO USE THEM CORRECTLY TO EFFECTIVELY CHANGE OUR WORLD FOR THE POSITIVE. WE HAVE THOUGHTS, WE HAVE SPEECH AND HOW TO CORRECTLY SPEAK THE WORDS, AND WE HAVE EXPERIENCING THE MANIFESTATION OF OUR CREATIONS. WHAT YOU ARE EXPERIENCING AT THIS EXACT MOMENT IS "THE AWARENESS", THE ANSWER TO YOUR QUESTION, "HOW CAN I TURN MY LIFE AROUND", OR "WHAT DOES IT TAKE FOR ME TO GET MY LIFE IN ORDER", OR THE BIG QUESTION ITSELF "WHAT AM I DOING HERE"? YOU ARE HERE TO EXPERIENCE EVERYTHING YOU WISH FOR. THE WIND IN YOUR HAIR, THE WARMTH OF THE SUN, THE COOLNESS OF A FALL DAY, THE EMBRACE OF ANOTHER HUMAN BEING. OUR SOUL IS "PURE POSITIVE" ENERGY AND AS "PURE POSITIVE" ENERGY WE CAN NOT FEEL THESE TYPES OF DIFFERENT ENERGIES IN OUR "PURE POSITIVE" SOUL ENERGY FORM. THIS IS THE PURPOSE OF THE BODY AS FLESH AND THE BRAIN TO INFORM OUR SOUL WHAT THESE OTHER ENERGY FORMS FEEL LIKE UPON US. THIS WAY WE CAN COMPARE OUR ENTITIES OF ENERGY. GOD HAS GIVEN YOU "THIS" AND YOU "ARE" GIVING TO GOD THE EXPERIENCES YOU ARE EXPERIENCING. IT IS THE PERFECT GIFT EXCHANGE.

GOD'S PURPOSE

IT IS WITHOUT LIMITS OR BOUNDARIES WHICH WE

PLACE UPON THYSELF

IT IS THE TRUEST FORM OF ENERGY THAT WE PLACE
UPON A SHELF

IT IS THERE FOR WHEN WE USE IT AND IS ALWAYS
USED IN FORM

IT IS PLACED UPON US, WHEN WE ARE FRESHLY BORN

TO USE THIS TYPE OF POWER WE ALWAYS SEE FIT

FOR THE FINAL END RESULT IS THE JOY DERIVED FROM
IT

WE SEEK GOD'S MIGHTY WISDOM THROUGH OUR PRAYERS
ON BENDED KNEES

WHAT WE ASK IS ALWAYS THERE SO SET YOUR MIND AT
EASE

WHAT WE LONG FOR TO DEFINE

OUR EXISTENCE THROUGHOUT TIME

THE DIFFERENCE WE CAN MAKE

IS TO LEARN FROM OUR MISTAKE

TO FEEL OUR EVER KNOWING

TO A PLACE WE ALL ARE GOING

TO A VOID OF EMPTY SPACE

TO OUR EXISTENCE IN THIS PLACE

GOD'S PURPOSE ALWAYS PRESENT WHERE TIME AND
SPACE DISSOLVE

TO EXPERIENCE THE DEFINING OF ALL THAT ARE
INVOLVED

GOD'S PURPOSE TO EXPERIENCE ALL GOD HAS CREATED

WHICH GIVES DEFINITION TO GOD'S PRESENCE THAT
CAN NOT BE DEBATED!

JOHN A. BOLDEN

AUGUST 7, 2004

NOW, IN RELIGION THESE THREE TOOLS ARE KNOWN AS,

"THE FATHER",

"THE SON",

AND,

 "THE HOLY GHOST".

IN SPIRITUALISM THEY ARE KNOWN AS

"MIND",

" BODY",

 AND

"SPIRIT".

EITHER WAY YOU KNOW OF THESE IT IS

"THINKING",

"SPEAKING",

AND

"EXPERIENCING".

18

"THE FATHER", DEFINING GOD EQUALS OUR THOUGHTS/THINKING.

"THE SON", DEFINING JESUS, EQUALS OUR SPEECH, FOR JESUS SPOKE VERBALLY "THE WORD" TO US ABOUT THIS VERY SAME THING.
"THE HOLY GHOST", IS OUR SOUL, "PURE POSITIVE ENERGY", WHICH IS EQUAL TO THE EXPERIENCING OF OUR CREATIONS, OUR MANIFESTATIONS. IF YOU ARE A BIBLE READER, PLACE THESE DIFFERENT DEFINITIONS WHERE YOU SEE THOSE THREE WORDS. FATHER, SON OR WORD, AND HOLY GHOST AND SEE WHAT YOU COME UP WITH. IT WILL NOT CHANGE THE DEFINITION OF THE BIBLE, AND THE TRANSLATION OF THE MESSAGE WILL BECOME MUCH CLEARER FOR YOU. LET'S TAKE A LOOK AT ENERGY AND HOW IT COMES INTO VIEW WITH MANIFESTATION OF CREATION.

ENERGY

EVERYTHING AND ANYTHING IS ENERGY. IT IS SOMETHING THAT CAN BE SEEN BUT MOST OF US CHOOSE NOT TO SEE IT. ALL MATTER IS ENERGY FORMED THROUGH MANIFESTATION. YOUR SOUL IS THE ENERGY ENCASED AROUND YOUR BODY. THIS IS "WHO YOU REALLY ARE". YOUR THOUGHTS ARE YOUR SOUL WHICH IN TURN IS "WHO YOU REALLY ARE". AS YOUR THOUGHT FORM TRAVELS, IT HAS A CERTAIN VIBRATION TO IT, A SIGNATURE. NOW, MIX THIS IN WITH THE UNIVERSAL LAW OF "LIKE ATTRACTS LIKE". WHEN YOU ASK FOR A CERTAIN EXPERIENCE TO ENTER INTO YOUR LIFE, YOUR THOUGHT FORM HAS THAT CERTAIN VIBRATIONAL FREQUENCY, FIRST STEP OF CREATION IS

"THOUGHT", NOW YOUR SPEECH PATTERN COMES INTO PLAY, WHEN YOU SPEAK IT OUT LOUD, THAT TO, HAS A CERTAIN VIBRATIONAL FREQUENCY, THESE TWO FREQUENCIES MIX TOGETHER TO FORM ONE CERTAIN VIBRATIONAL FREQUENCY. THIS IS SENT OUT INTO THE UNIVERSE SEEKING WHAT YOU ARE WISHING TO EXPERIENCE. WHEN THIS FREQUENCY FINDS A MATCH TO IT, THEN THE POWERS OF THE UNIVERSE START TO BRING THESE TOGETHER. YOU START TO MEET PEOPLE WHO GIVE YOU MESSAGES ON WHERE TO OBTAIN MORE INFORMATION ON HOW TO REACH THAT EXPERIENCE. THEY LEAD YOU TO BOOKS, MOVIES, TV SHOWS, RADIO CHANNELS TO LISTEN TO, SONGS, POEMS, ANYTHING AND EVERYTHING COMES TO YOU TO HELP YOU TO REACH THAT EXPERIENCE. GOD SEND US NOTHING BUT ANGELS INTO OUR LIFE. THE MOST IMPORTANT ONE IS THAT INNER VOICE, THAT INNER FEELING MOST OF US WILL DECIDE TO LISTEN TO, FROM NOW ON, QUITE OFTEN. AS I SIT HERE AND WRITE THAT COMMENT, WHAT JUST HAPPENED TO ME, WAS MY INABILITY TO CONTINUE TO WRITE THIS MESSAGE TO YOU. MY ABILITY TO LISTEN WAS HINDERED JUST BY WRITING THAT STATEMENT.

I AM "THANKFUL" FOR THAT EXPERIENCE, AND IT NO LONGER SERVES ME.

THAT IS HOW ENERGY WORKS, SOMETIMES MANIFESTATION OF CREATION IS INSTANT, SOMETIMES IT TAKES YEARS. KNOWING HOW TO CREATE INSTANTLY IS THE KEY TO MASTERY AND KNOWING THAT CREATION IS INSTANT IS MASTERY. KNOWING THAT I JUST CREATED THAT SMALL MENTAL BLOCK, I THANK IT FOR THE EXPERIENCE AND CLAIM IT AS MINE. IT NO LONGER SERVES ME WITH IT'S PURPOSE, GOD BLESS IT

AS I SEND IT OUT INTO THE UNIVERSE.

"WHAT WE RESIST, SHALL PERSIST".

CLAIM YOUR CREATION WITH LOVE, NOT HATRED. THE ENERGY OF HATRED IS A CONSTANT TWIRLING MOTION OF EMOTION. IT IS YOUR RESISTANCE OF YOUR ACCEPTANCE OF YOUR CREATION OF IT THAT STAYS WITH YOU. HATRED MUST HAVE YOUR LOVE, YOUR ACCEPTANCE OF IT'S CREATION, IN ORDER FOR IT TO DISSIPATE.

THIS IS THE ESSENCE OF FORGIVING.

FORGIVING IS NOT EXCUSING SOMEONE OR SOMETHING FOR THEIR NEGATIVE ACTIONS OR THOUGHTS. FORGIVING IS " FOR GIVING" YOUR ENERGY, YOUR ENERGY OF LOVE AND ACCEPTANCE OF YOUR CREATION. YOU HAVE TO CLAIM OWNERSHIP, ACCEPT THE RESPONSIBILITY FOR HAVING CREATED AND CO-CREATED THAT CERTAIN INSTANCE OF YOUR LIFE. WHEN YOU REALIZE THIS, WHEN YOU COME TO ACCEPT THIS AS YOU, YOU WILL COME TO LOVE YOURSELF, THEN LOVING EVERYONE AROUND YOU BECOMES EASY. NEGATIVITY IS AN ESSENCE, AN ENTITY THAT WE CREATE.

NEGATIVITY

AS YOU LIE AWAKE IN DEEP DESPAIR
EMOTIONLESS HEART ONE CAN NOT REPAIR

PAIN AND SUFFERING IS THE LIFE YOU LEAD
ALWAYS WANTING FOR THIS NEED
FOR HAPPINESS IT HURTS TOO MUCH
MORE POWER LIVES IN A NEGATIVE TOUCH
GO BEYOND THE LIGHTED TRAIL
INTO THE DARKENED PATH YOU HAIL
POWER, LUST, AND GREED FOR SURE
SEEMS TO MAKE ONES LIFE SO CLEAN AND PURE
YOUR EYES SEE NOT WHAT YOU CAN BE
ENLIGHTENED HEART AND MIND SO FREE
CAST INTO PRISON MADE OF YOUR OWN
SITTING ON A SELF MADE THRONE
FOR THERE YOU ARE THE KING OF WIT
PUTS DOWN THE PEOPLE WITH THE WORDS YOU SPIT
THE CLOUDS LINED HEAVY WITH THE THOUGHTLESS SOUL
FROM THOSE YOU BANISHED TO MAKE YOU WHOLE
ONE DAY SOON YOU SHALL SEE
THE POWER OF LIGHT LIVES WITHIN THEE!

WHEN A PERSON FALLS INTO A DEPRESSION, IT SEEMS TO THEM THAT ALL IS NEGATIVE WITHIN THEIR WORLD, AND THIS IS SO VERY TRUE, WHY?, YOU ASK, BECAUSE THEY HAVE CREATED IT SO, WHY, WOULD SOMEONE DO THAT?, BECAUSE WE CAN NOT KNOW TRUE HAPPINESS UNLESS WE KNOW TRUE SADNESS. THIS IS WHAT THE BRAIN AND BODY IS FOR, TO INTERPRET THESE EXPERIENCES AS WE FEEL THEM. NOW THE PROBLEM THAT LIES,

NOTE{ATTENTION THE WORD "LIES" IN THE SENTENCE, THE FEELING THAT I AM DESCRIBING TO YOU IS A LIE ABOUT "WHO YOU REALLY ARE", "YOU ARE NOT NEGATIVE ENERGY", "YOU ARE PURE POSITIVE ENERGY EXPERIENCING NEGATIVE ENERGY SO THAT YOU MAY TRULY KNOW YOU ARE PURE POSITIVE ENERGY".}

WITHIN IS THE ACCEPTANCE OF THE CREATION OF THESE TWO STRONG ENTITIES. BASICALLY, THE MAJORITY OF US ACCEPT AND CLAIM OWNERSHIP OF HAPPINESS, IT CREATES US TO FEEL GOOD AND HELPS TO PRODUCE HAPPINESS IN THOSE AROUND US. IT BUILDS OUR EGO WITH STRENGTH AND COURAGE. THEREFOR THE ACCEPTANCE OF HAPPINESS AS OUR CREATION IS THE LOVE THAT WE GIVE TO IT, UNLESS WE DON'T. THIS IS WHERE THINGS CAN GET A LITTLE CONFUSING. TAKE A STROLL DOWN MEMORY LANE FOR A MOMENT TO A DAY THAT IS FABULOUS. YOU ARE FEELING FANTASTIC, EVERYONE AROUND YOU IS FEELING FANTASTIC. YOU SAY IN YOUR MIND, YOUR THOUGHTS, GOD THIS IS A GREAT DAY, I FEEL WONDERFUL. YOU ARE THANKFUL FOR THIS. YOUR THOUGHTS ARE POSITIVE, FIRST LEVEL OF CREATION {THOUGHTS}, NOW YOU EXPRESS THIS TO SOMEONE IN A CASUAL CONVERSATION.

"GOD, I'M FEELING GOOD TODAY!"

OR SOMEONE ASKS YOU,

"HOW ARE YOU FEELING TODAY?",

"HOW ARE YOU TODAY?"

YOUR RESPONSE, BACK IN SPEECH,

"I'M FEELING GREAT!, THANK YOU!"

SECOND LEVEL OF CREATION, SPEAKING OF IT. NOW
YOU HAVE JUST CLAIMED OWNERSHIP OF YOUR
HAPPINESS CREATION. THIRD LEVEL OF CREATION IS
EXPERIENCING THAT HAPPINESS FEELING YOU CREATED
FOR YOURSELF. YOU HAVE CLAIMED OWNERSHIP AND
SHOWED "THANKFULNESS" FOR IT'S EXISTENCE.
HAPPINESS CAN LEAVE YOU AT ANYTIME YOU WISH IT
TO LEAVE NOW. WHEN YOU DECIDE IT NO LONGER
SERVES YOU. NOW, LET'S LOOK AT THE ENERGY
INVOLVED WHEN YOU GIVE A POSITIVE RESPONSE TO
THAT SAME QUESTION,

"HOW ARE YOU TODAY?",

WHEN YOU ARE FEELING NOT SO POSITIVE INSIDE. MOST
OF US WILL EXPRESS, IN SPEECH, TO OTHER PEOPLE OUR
HAPPINESS EVEN THOUGH WE ARE FEELING HO HUM
THAT DAY, SO AS TO AVOID BRINGING THE OTHER
PERSON DOWN OR FOR JUST HIDING OUR TRUE
FEELINGS, COMMON COURTESY AND SOLITUDE CAN GO
HAND IN HAND SOMETIMES. YOU EXPRESS

"I AM FINE, THANK YOU."

EVEN THOUGH YOU FEEL HO HUM AND YOU KNOW THAT
YOU ARE, BECAUSE YOU ARE THINKING ABOUT IT, BUT
YOU EXPRESSED FEELING FINE AND BEING THANKFUL
FOR IT, POSITIVE ENERGY DOES NOT PRESENT IT SELF
FOR THE REASON OF BEING THANKFUL FOR IT'S
PRESENCE. POSITIVE ENERGY, TRUE HAPPINESS, CAN
NOT ENTER INTO YOU, BECAUSE TO YOU IT NO LONGER

SERVES YOU, WHAT SERVES YOU AT THE TIME IS THE HO HUM FEELING AND THAT WILL NOT LEAVE YOU UNLESS YOU ARE THANKFUL AND LOVING OF IT'S NATURE THAT YOU HAVE CREATED. THAT IS THE ESSENCE OF "UNLESS IT'S NOT." IN THOSE CASES IT IS BEST NOT TO SAY ANYTHING AT ALL WHICH IS THE ESSENCE OF

"SUFFERING IN SILENCE",

AND WILL BE CHANGED TO

"BEING HAPPY IN SILENCE",

BECAUSE NOW YOU KNOW WHAT EFFECTS "SAYING WORDS" HAVE UPON YOUR EXPERIENCES/FEELINGS. THIS IS WHAT MONKS, PRIESTS, BUDDHISTS, AND OTHER RELIGIONS PRACTICE TO GIVE THEM THE DISCIPLINE FOR

"NOT SAYING THE WRONG THING."

AS WE ALREADY KNOW THERE IS NOTHING WRONG NOR RIGHT, THERE IS ONLY EXPERIENCE. THOUGH, NOT SAYING ANYTHING AT ALL HAS IT'S ADVANTAGES, IF IT IS PRACTICED FOR A LONG PERIOD OF TIME, IT TAKES AWAY THE ESSENCE OF EXPERIENCING HOW WE CAN CONSCIOUSLY CREATE OUR WORLD. IT WOULD GIVE TO US THE ESSENCE OF EXISTING, BUT NOT LIVING. IT WOULD TAKE AWAY FROM OUR ABILITY TO MANIFEST AND EXPERIENCE OUR CREATIONS, BUT ON THE OTHER HAND, THE

"UNLESS IT'S NOT"

PORTION, WOULD GIVE TO US THE EXPERIENCE OF ONLY

EXISTING. WHICH ONE WOULD SERVE YOU BETTER?

"WHY AND HOW WOULD I LET SOMETHING AS GREAT AS HAPPINESS LEAVE ME?"

THE ANSWER AGAIN IS, "YOU CAN NOT REMEMBER HAPPINESS IF YOU DO NOT REMEMBER SADNESS". THEY ARE THE SAME ENTITIES ON THE DIFFERENT SIDES OF THE SPECTRUM. THAT'S THE

"WHY",

THE

"HOW"

IS A DIFFICULT TASK TO SEE IF YOU DO NOT KNOW WHAT YOU ARE LOOKING FOR. LET'S TAKE THAT SAME CASUAL CONVERSATION.

"HOW ARE YOU TODAY?",

"I'M FANTASTIC, THANK YOU.",

"HOW ABOUT YOURSELF?",

"I'M FEELING A BIT ON THE LOW SIDE, KIND OF TIRED, YOU KNOW?",

"YES, I KNOW WHAT YOU MEAN."

LOOK AT THAT LAST STATEMENT,

"YES, I KNOW WHAT YOU MEAN.

YOU HAVE JUST DECLARED THAT YOU ARE
KNOWLEDGEABLE INTO THAT PERSONS
"MEANNESS"

AND

"YES, YOU ALSO DECLARED THE ACCEPTANCE OF THAT
PERSONS ENERGY INTO YOUR LIFE.

THEY HAVE JUST GIVEN TO YOU THEIR LOW SIDE AND
KIND OF TIRED FEELING AND YES, YOU ALREADY KNOW
IT'S COMING BECAUSE YOU DECLARED

"YES, I KNOW WHAT, YOU ARE MEAN".

NOW YOUR MIND STARTS THINKING THOUGHTS OF
SADNESS,

"I FEEL BAD FOR SO AND SO".

YOU MEET SOMEONE ELSE AND START A CONVERSATION
WITH THEM.

"HAVE YOU SEEN SO AND SO TODAY, GOD, I FEEL BAD
FOR THEM",

BOOM, YOU'VE JUST CREATED THAT ENERGY SO GIVE IT
A LITTLE TIME AND IT WILL MANIFEST INTO YOUR
CREATION, MOST LIKELY BY LATE AFTERNOON OR THE
NEXT DAY!
    TO WARD OFF SUCH NEGATIVITY AND TO "WILL THEM
AND YOU TO HAVE A BETTER DAY, WILL BE TO SAY,

"THINGS ARE MUCH BRIGHTER IN YOUR LIFE THAN YOU
THINK!"

FOR WHAT YOU SPEAK TO THEM YOU ACTUALLY SPEAK TO YOURSELF. THIS IS WHAT TO LOOK FOR IN YOUR SPEECH PATTERNS AND THOUGHT PATTERNS. YOUR COMPASSION FOR PEOPLE IS NOT A DOWNFALL IN YOUR LIFE, COMPASSION IS A BEAUTIFUL THING, IT IS LOVE EXPRESSED, IT IS HOW YOU EXPRESS IT THAT EFFECTS YOUR WORLD. KEEP IT POSITIVE ON YOUR EXPRESSIONS AND OTHERS NEGATIVITY WILL NOT HELP YOU CREATE NEGATIVITY IN YOUR WORLD. WHEN YOU TALK ABOUT SOMEONE, YOU ARE, IN REALITY, TALKING ABOUT YOURSELF. THIS IS WHY WE WILL NOT JUDGE OTHERS BY THEIR APPEARANCE OR ACTIONS.

"JUDGE NOT, LESS THEE BE JUDGED!"

THINK OF THIS MESSAGE IN TERMS OF CREATION OF YOUR WORLD.

"THINK IT",

"SPEAK IT",

"EXPERIENCE IT".

IF YOU JUDGE ANOTHER PERSON YOU ARE FORMING OPINIONS IN YOUR MIND ABOUT THEM, YOUR THOUGHTS, FIRST LEVEL OF CREATION. THEN YOU START TALKING ABOUT THEM, YOUR SPEECH, SECOND LEVEL OF CREATION. THE ONLY THING LEFT IS TO EXPERIENCE EXACTLY WHAT YOU JUDGED THAT OTHER PERSON TO BE. YOU CREATED, FOR YOURSELF, THAT EXACT SAME VERSION OF THE PERSON YOU HAVE JUDGED. THEN WHAT HAPPENS AFTER THAT? YOU START TO BLAME THAT PERSON, YOU JUDGED, FOR THE

28

NEGATIVITY THAT SURROUNDS YOUR WORLD. THE
HATRED FOR THEM BUILDS UP INSIDE YOU MORE AND
MORE, THEN CONFRONTATION COMES IN, DEPENDING
ON HOW CREATIVE YOU ARE IN THAT DEPARTMENT.
NOW,

"HOW DO YOU DISSOLVE A SITUATION LIKE THIS"?

 FIRST OF ALL,

"STOP JUDGING OTHERS"!

KNOW THAT THEY ARE ON A GREAT SPIRITUAL
JOURNEY, AS YOU ARE, OF EXPERIENCE AND OF
REMEMBERING

"WHO THEY REALLY ARE."

YOU INVITED THEM INTO YOUR LIFE TO HELP WITH
YOUR JOURNEY AS WELL. THEY ARE YOUR CREATION
ALSO. SECOND, CLAIM RESPONSIBILITY FOR CREATING
THAT NEGATIVITY IN YOUR WORLD, IT IS, IN ALL
ACTUALITY, YOUR CREATION! IT WAS NURTURED BY
YOU, RAISED BY YOU, AND MATURED BY YOU! ACCEPT IT,
LOVE IT, AND BLESS IT FOR THE EXPERIENCE IT HAS
GIVEN YOU, IF IT NO LONGER SERVES YOU, SEND IT BACK
OUT INTO THE UNIVERSE WITH GOD'S BLESSING. THEN
CREATE A NEW EXPERIENCE, A MUCH MORE HAPPIER,
POSITIVE LIFE. HOW DO YOU DO THIS? LET'S CLARIFY
THAT STATEMENT OF

"JUDGE NOT, LESS THEE BE JUDGED".

IF YOU DO NOT EXPRESS NEGATIVITY OF ANOTHER
INDIVIDUAL OR GROUP, YOU DO NOT EXPRESS

NEGATIVITY WITHIN YOURSELF. IF YOU DO NOT EXPRESS LIMITATIONS OF A PERSON OR GROUP, YOU DO NOT CREATE LIMITATIONS UPON YOURSELF. THIS LEADS US INTO THE PHRASE OF

"GOD HELPS THOSE WHO HELP THEMSELVES."

GOD HELPS THOSE WHO HELP THEMSELVES

HOW DO WE CREATE A MORE POSITIVE LIFE AFTER THE EXPERIENCE OF JUDGING ANOTHER? TAKE EXACTLY WHAT YOU ARE REMEMBERING HERE ON HOW TO CONSCIOUSLY CREATE YOUR WORLD AND SHARE IT WITH THAT INDIVIDUAL OR GROUP. WE TEACH WHAT WE ARE LEARNING. WHEN YOU HELP SOMEONE REMEMBER "WHO THEY REALLY ARE" YOU ARE HELPING YOURSELF REMEMBER "WHO YOU REALLY ARE." YOU HAVE BEEN BROUGHT TOGETHER BY THE CREATION OF YOUR WORLD. REMEMBER

"GOD SENDS US NOTHING BUT ANGELS."

EVERY PERSON, PLACE, OR THING YOU COME INTO CONTACT WITH HAS A MESSAGE FOR YOU. IT IS WHEN, "YOU DECIDE TO LISTEN TO WHAT IS BEING EXPRESSED TO YOU, THAT YOU FINALLY GET THE DEFINITION OF THE ANSWER TO YOUR QUESTION,

"THAT IS DEFINING YOU",

SO THAT YOU CAN MOVE FORWARD TOWARDS YOUR

GOAL OF ONENESS WITH GOD,

"YOUR SPIRITUAL EVOLUTION".

"HOW DID THIS PERSON ENTER INTO MY LIFE"?

"HOW DID I CREATE SUCH A PRESENCE"?

IF YOU THINK BACK AT A TIME IN YOUR LIFE, WHEN YOU MAY HAVE THOUGHT,

"HOW CAN I HELP SOMEONE OR YOURSELF BE A BETTER PERSON?",

OR ANYTHING TO THAT DEGREE OF QUESTIONING THOUGHTS AND THEN SPOKE THE QUESTION OUT LOUD TO SOMEONE, IN YOUR MIND, AT THE TIME, YOU MAY HAVE MEANT ONLY ONE PERSON. YOU MAY HAVE NOT BEEN SPECIFIC IN YOUR ASKING. SO YOU SAY,

"HOW CAN I HELP?"

THE ENERGY OF THIS IS SENT OUT INTO THE UNIVERSE AND STARTS TO MANIFEST INTO EXPERIENCE. YOU HELP THAT ONE PERSON AND FEEL GOOD ABOUT IT. THEN ANOTHER PERSON SHOWS UP ASKING FOR YOUR HELP, YOU DO IT, YOU'RE FEELING OK ABOUT IT, THEN ANOTHER ASKS FOR YOUR HELP. ENERGY OF MANIFESTATION IS ALWAYS INTO PLAY. YOU ASK YOURSELF

"WHEN IS THIS GOING TO STOP?, I HAVE THINGS OF MY OWN TO DO AND I DON'T SEE ANYONE ASKING ME IF I NEED HELP."

YOU DIDN'T ASK FOR HELP, YOU ASKED TO BE THE HELPER. WHICH IS WHAT YOU BECAME. YOU HAVEN'T CLOSED THAT MANIFESTATION OF BEING THE HELPER. YOU MUST, AGAIN, CLAIM OWNERSHIP OF YOUR CREATION, BE THANKFUL FOR THE EXPERIENCE, BLESS IT WITH GOD'S LOVE, LOVE IT WITH YOUR LOVE, AND SEND IT BACK OUT INTO THE UNIVERSE.

THE REASON NO ONE IS ASKING IF YOU COULD USE SOME HELP IS BECAUSE OF YOUR EXPRESSION OF " I DON'T SEE ANYONE ASKING IF I NEED HELP."

YOU HAVE EXPRESSED THE NEEDINESS AND WANTINGNESS OF HELP, THERE FOR THAT IS WHAT YOU SHALL RECEIVE, NEEDINESS AND WANTINGNESS. NOW, THIS GOES HAND IN HAND WITH SOMEONE SAYING,

"I NEED YOUR HELP"

 OR

"I WANT YOUR HELP."

THE NEXT TIME SOMEONE SAYS THIS TO YOU, FEEL THE ENERGY THAT SURROUNDS YOU AND HOW IT PUSHES YOU AWAY AND HOW YOU BECOME DEFENSIVE IN YOUR MIND, THE WAY YOU REACT TO IT. YOUR ENERGY LEVEL STARTS TO DRAIN, YOU START COMING UP WITH EXCUSES ON WHY YOU CAN'T HELP. THEY AREN'T ASKING FOR YOUR HELP, THEY ARE ASKING FOR THE NEEDINESS AND WANTINGNESS OF YOUR HELP, THEN WHEN YOU ARE UNABLE TO HELP THEM, THEY GET MAD AT YOU. FOR THEY SEEK TO FEEL THE EXPERIENCE OF ANGER AND THAT IS WHAT YOU SHALL GIVE TO THEM. WHY?, BECAUSE THE UNIVERSE GIVES TO US

EVERYTHING WE ASK FOR. TEACH TO THEM WHAT YOU
ARE REMEMBERING HERE AND LIFE WILL BE MUCH
SMOOTHER FOR EVERYONE INVOLVED.

JESUS TEACHES US TO CHANGE NEGATIVITY

AS I WRITE THIS BOOK, I HAVE COME ACROSS MANY
STUMBLING BLOCKS OF EXPRESSION. THESE BLOCKS
INCLUDE HEADACHES, HEALTH PROBLEMS,
PROCRASTINATION, LACK OF ENERGY, AND NOT
KNOWING WHAT TO WRITE. AS YOU READ THIS BOOK
YOU MAY FEEL THESE VERY SAME THINGS, OR YOU MAY
NOT. THE EXPRESSION OF NEGATIVITY MUST BE
CONFRONTED IN ORDER TO CHANGE IT. I CLAIM THE
CREATION OF THIS ENTITY, I AM THANKFUL FOR THE
EXPERIENCE, I EMBRACE IT WITH MY LOVE, AND BLESS
IT WITH THE GRACE OF GOD, AS I SEND IT BACK INTO
THE UNIVERSE. THIS IS WHAT JESUS WAS TRYING TO
TEACH US. HE TRIED TO REACH THE MASSES OF PEOPLE
AND HOW TO CONSCIOUSLY CREATE THEIR WORLD. TO
BEAUTIFY THEIR WORLD WITH POSITIVITY AND THE
ONLY WAY TO DO THIS, IS TO ACCEPT WITH LOVE THE
NEGATIVITY OF OUR LIFE THAT WE CREATED. LOVE IT,
BE THANKFUL FOR IT'S EXPERIENCE, BLESS THE
EXPERIENCE, AND LET NEGATIVITY KNOW

"IT NO LONGER SERVES OUR PURPOSE",

AND RELEASE IT BACK OUT INTO THE UNIVERSE. WHEN
JESUS SAW THAT HE WAS ONLY REACHING A FEW
PEOPLE, HE KNEW WHAT HE HAD TO DO. HE HAD TO

CREATE A NEGATIVE SITUATION, FOR ALL TO SEE AND
TO REMEMBER TILL THIS VERY DAY. JESUS CAME DOWN
TO A LEVEL OF EDUCATION FOR THE MASSES. HE WAS
SHOWING TO EVERYONE TO ACCEPT, LOVE, BE
THANKFUL, BE BLESSED TOWARDS NEGATIVITY, AND
RELEASE IT BACK INTO THE UNIVERSE. THEN YOU CAN
SEE THE LIGHT OF LOVE AFTER THE REIGN OF
DARKNESS HAS LEFT. THIS IS WHEN YOU CAN BUILD A
LIFE OF POSITIVE HAPPINESS. THIS IS WHAT JESUS LEFT
US WITHIN OUR WORLD AND FOR THAT I AM VERY
"APPRECIATIVE" OF. IT SERVES US WITH SUCH LOVE AND
HAPPINESS TOWARDS LIFE THAT WE WILL FOREVER
KEEP IT IN OUR LIFE.

"OK, SO, IF JESUS CREATED AND ACCEPTED THIS
NEGATIVITY, HE COULD HAVE LOVED IT, BLESSED IT,
AND SENT IT BACK INTO THE UNIVERSE, HE COULD HAVE
STOPPED IT AT ANYTIME, CORRECT?" YES, HE COULD
HAVE, AND JESUS TOOK IT ONE STEP FURTHER TO SHOW
US

"NOT TO FEAR OUR CREATION OF NEGATIVITY".

TO FEAR OUR CREATIONS, IS TO DENY OUR CREATIONS,
WHICH IS IN TURN, DENIAL OF "WHO WE REALLY ARE."
JESUS WAS TEACHING US NOT TO FEAR DEATH BECAUSE
WE NEVER REALLY DIE, WE CHANGE OUR FORM BACK
INTO

"PURE POSITIVE ENERGY",

"OUR SOUL".

THERE IS NOTHING TO FEAR OR BE AFRAID OF WHEN
YOU CONSCIOUSLY CREATE YOUR WORLD. YOUR SOUL
WILL NOT LET GO OF THE BODY AND MIND UNTIL YOUR
SOUL,"WHO YOU REALLY ARE", DECIDES IT IS TIME TO

CHANGE FORM, WHICH LEADS US INTO A DISCUSSION
ABOUT DEATH OF THE BODY.

CHANGING FORM/DEATH OF THE BODY

OUR LIFE IS FULL OF CONSTANT CHANGE, AS WE
ALREADY KNOW THIS. EVERY TIME YOU THINK OF
DYING, EVERY TIME YOU TALK OF DYING, YOU START
MANIFESTING THE AGING PROCESS. SO, THEN, IF THIS IS
TRUE AND IF WE WISH TO REMAIN YOUNG AND VIBRANT
THEN WE WILL NEVER HAVE TO LEAVE THIS WORLD
AND STAY ATTACHED TO THE BODY? THE ANSWER TO
THAT QUESTION IS MOST DEFINITELY,
"YES, WE CAN",

WHEN WE SO DESIRE TO DO SO! IF YOU THINK THIS IS
NOT TRUE, THEN YOU HAVE JUST ADDED TO YOUR
AGING PROCESS, SO THINK AGAIN! I HAVE READ AND
HEARD THAT OUR BODIES ARE UNABLE TO DO SO
BECAUSE THE CELLS IN OUR CENTRAL NERVOUS
SYSTEM DO NOT REPRODUCE OR REGENERATE
THEMSELVES. AFTER HEALING MY BODY AND SOUL I
WILL HAVE TO DISAGREE WITH THAT. WHEN WE CAN
VISIBLY SEE OUR BODY HEAL QUICKLY FROM A CUT OR
WOUND EXTERNALLY THEN WE ALSO DO KNOW THAT
OUR ORGANS WITHIN OUR BODY HEAL QUICKLY,
INTERNALLY, AS WELL. EVER WONDER WHY SOMEONE
WHO IS 60 LOOKS LIKE THEY ARE 40 AND SOMEONE WHO
IS 40 LOOKS LIKE THEY ARE 60. STUDY THOSE PEOPLE,
WHEN YOU CAN. LISTEN TO THEIR SPEECH AND HOW
THEY PRESENT THEMSELVES AND HOW THEY TALK OF
OTHERS. YOU WILL SEE EXACTLY HOW THE ENERGY OF

POSITIVITY AND NEGATIVITY WORK. WE ALL HAVE OUR
UPS AND DOWNS AND NOW YOU KNOW HOW THIS
WORKS. LET'S GET INTO A LITTLE MORE DETAIL OF
THIS. WHEN NEGATIVITY SURROUNDS A PERSON AND
THE MORE INTENSE IT GETS AND MOVES INTO
DEPRESSION. THEY THINK OF SUICIDE, THEY TALK OF
SUICIDE, EITHER OF DOING THEIR OWN OR TALKING OF
ANOTHER, THE ENERGY STARTS TO MANIFEST. LIFE
ENERGY STARTS TO DWINDLE DOWN REINFORCING THE
DEPRESSION, THAT PERSON'S FREQUENCY STARTS TO
SLOW DOWN.

UNIVERSAL LAW "LIKE ATTRACTS LIKE".

THAT FREQUENCY STARTS TO ATTRACT DISEASE, NOW
GIVE ATTENTION TOTHIS WORD

"DIS / EASE".

DISEASE IS CAUSED BY TWO ENTITIES IN LIFE.
PARASITES AND BAD BACTERIA. THAT LOW ENERGY
FREQUENCY DEPRESSED PEOPLE TRANSMIT INVITES
THESE LOW FREQUENCY PARASITES AND BAD BACTERIA
INTO THE BODY. THEY ARE MICROSCOPIC AT FIRST
THEN THEY GROW INTO ADULTS. THINK OF HOW WE AS
HUMAN BEINGS STARTED OUT AND HOW BIG WE GET. I
BELIEVE YOU GET THE PICTURE. HERE IS AN EXAMPLE
OF HOW THIS MAY START. YOU KNOW OF SOMEONE
WHO HAS A SICKNESS, DOESN'T HAVE TO BE A SERIOUS
ONE, MAYBE JUST A COMMON COLD, YOU START
THINKING ABOUT IT AND HOPE THAT YOU WILL NOT
CATCH IT, YOU ARE THINKING ABOUT IT CONSTANTLY
AND WONDER WHY YOU CAN'T STOP THINKING ABOUT
IT, THEN A FRIEND SHOWS UP AND YOU START TALKING
ABOUT IT TO THEM.

"DON'T GO OVER TO SEE SO AND SO, THEY HAVE A COLD AND I AM HOPING I DON'T CATCH IT."
IN A WAY YOU ARE WARDING OFF THIS COLD BUT IN ANOTHER YOU ARE NOT. OF COURSE THE CONVERSATION GOES ON ABOUT OTHERS HAVING IT AND THEN ONTO SOMETHING ELSE. AFTER AWHILE YOU GET A LITTLE HUNGRY YOU BRING OUT SOME CHEESE AND CRACKERS AND MEAT OR PULL OUT SOME CHIPS AND DIP AND THE DIP HAS BEEN IN THE REFRIGERATOR FOR A COUPLE WEEKS OR AFTER YOU GET DONE MUNCHING ON THE OPEN PLATE OF MUNCHIES YOU FORGET TO COVER THEM UP AND PLACE THEM BACK INTO THE REFRIGERATOR. SOMEONE ELSE SHOWS UP THEN ANOTHER AND THE PLATE OF MUNCHIES IS STILL OPEN. THEN AFTER EVERYONE LEAVES YOU START TO CLEAN UP, YOU SEE THE PLATE OF MUNCHIES AND BECOME A LITTLE HUNGRY. NOW THIS PLATE HAS BEEN SITTING OUT IN THE OPEN COLLECTING DUST AND DUST MITES AND OTHER THINGS FOR A COUPLE HOURS OR MORE AND NOW YOU ARE FEELING HUNGRY AND MUNCHING ON THIS. THE NEXT MORNING YOU FEEL THE COLD COMING ON AND START TO BLAME THAT OTHER PERSON YOU MET AND TALKED ABOUT FOR GIVING YOU THE COLD, WHEN IN FACT THAT PERSON DIDN'T GIVE IT TO YOU, YOU CREATED IT FOR YOURSELF, JUST BY THINKING ABOUT IT AND THEN TALKING ABOUT IT, WHICH IN TURN ATTRACTED YOU TO THE OPEN PLATE OF MUNCHIES OR THE DIP THAT HAD ALREADY BEEN OPENED FOR A WEEK AND A HALF SITTING IN YOUR REFRIGERATOR. IF YOU HAD NOT CREATED THE FREQUENCY OF DISEASE YOU WOULD NOT HAVE FELT HUNGRY FOR THAT OPEN PLATE OF MUNCHIES AFTER EVERYONE HAD LEFT OR YOU WILL HAVE THROWN THEM AWAY OR WILL HAVE COVERED THEM UP, AFTER UTILIZING THEM AND PLACED THEM BACK INTO THE REFRIGERATOR AFTER EVERYONE WAS DONE EATING

THEM. I BELIEVE YOU SEE HOW THE ENERGY WORKS THERE. LET'S GET BACK TO CHANGING FORM.

WHEN WE ARE YOUNG AND GROWING, THERE IS A LOT OF ENERGY, THE IMMUNE SYSTEM IS VERY ACTIVE AND COURAGEOUSLY FIGHTS OFF THESE PARASITES AND BAD BACTERIA. MOST OF US ARE RAISED IN GOOD HEALTH PATTERNS, EATING THE RIGHT FOODS TO KEEP US HEALTHY. AS WE GROW OLDER WE PICK FOODS THAT ARE FASTER AND THE LEAST HEALTHY FOR US AND THE WASHING HABITS CHANGE.

"WE GET PARASITES AND BAD BACTERIA FROM THE FOOD WE EATAND THE WATER WE DRINK."

NOW OUR LIFESTYLE HAS CHANGED, THE MANIFESTATION OF OUR CREATION STARTS TO TAKE SHAPE, IT ALWAYS HAS BEEN. THE PEOPLE YOU WORK WITH, PARTY WITH, LIVE WITH, GET ALONG WITH, ALL ARE AT THE SAME FREQUENCY YOU ARE, JUST ABOUT.

"LIKE ATTRACTS LIKE".

YOU START THINKING ABOUT YOUR HEALTH AND HOW IT IS DETERIORATING, OF COURSE, YOU START TALKING ABOUT IT, MOST LIKELY IN A HUMOUROUS WAY, WHICH DEFINES, MORE CREATION OF MANIFESTATION ONLY TO INCREASE IT IN INTENSITY. EVERYTHING IS ALMOST FUNNY, BUT INSIDE, YOUR THOUGHTS, YOU KNOW IT ISN'T. YOUR THOUGHTS START WONDERING AS DO YOUR FRIENDS ABOUT WHAT IS HAPPENING, YOUR ENERGY MIXES, THE TENSION BUILDS, NEXT THING YOU KNOW, THERE IS AN ARGUMENT, AND SEPARATION. BLAMING EACH OTHER FOR THE REASON OF YOUR AILMENTS.

I CAN BEST EXPLAIN THIS THROUGH EXPRESSION OF AN EXPERIENCE OF MY LIFE, AND I BELIEVE MANY OF YOU CAN RELATE TO THIS. AS A YOUNG MAN GROWING

UP, I COULD SENSE MY FATHER'S HATRED FOR BEING TIED DOWN TO US AS A FAMILY. HE WAS MOSTLY GRUMPY AND FILLED WITH DISLIKE OF HIS LIFE. IT WAS APPARENT THROUGH HIS DRINKING AND ALCOHOLISM. HE "WANTED" HIS FREEDOM FOR HIS SINGLE LIFE. MY SISTER AND I "WANTED" HIM TO LEAVE. MY MOTHER LOVED HIM SO MUCH THAT SHE CATERED TO HIS EVERY "WISH" AND "WISHED" HIM TO REMAIN WITH US. SHE WAS A VERY POWERFUL BEAUTIFUL HUMAN AND SPIRITUAL BEING FILLED WITH LOVE. WHO ACCEPTED HIS ABUSE OF HER. SHE "WANTED" MY FATHER TO LOVE HER BACK THE WAY SHE LOVED HIM. AS I LOOK BACK UPON THIS SITUATION, I SEE AND KNOW THAT IT WAS THE MOST PERFECT CREATION THAT WAS CREATED. WE ALL GOT WHAT WE "WANTED". WE ALL RECEIVED THE "WANTINGNESS" WE ALL "WISHED" FOR WITH ALL OF OUR NEGATIVE ENERGY FLOWING AT EACH OTHER. IT WAS PUSHING ALL OF US AWAY FROM EACH OTHER, EXCEPT FOR THAT ONE KEY ENERGY THAT KEPT US ALL TOGETHER THROUGHOUT OUR GROWING YEARS. OUR "MOTHER'S LOVE" FOR EACH AND EVERYONE OF US. THE STRENGTH AND POWER OF LOVE OF ONE PERSON CAN HOLD BACK SUCH NEGATIVITY FROM MANY PEOPLE, NO MATTER HOW NEGATIVE THE SITUATION.

NOTE "GIVE CLOSE ATTENTION TO MY WORDS AS YOU READ THEM".

THE MORE MY SISTER AND I

"WANTED"

OUR FATHER "OUR THOUGHTS" TO LEAVE,

THE MORE HATRED MY FATHER {MY THOUGHTS} HAD

FOR HIMSELF {FOR MYSELF}

FOR BEING TIED DOWN TO HIS FAMILY AND HATING US FOR HATING HIM.

THE DESIRE OF WANTING IS INCREASED BECAUSE THIS IS WHAT WE WERE ACTUALLY WISHING FOR. THE WANTINGNESS OF THE WHOLE THING. HIS ANGER WAS EVEN MULTIPLIED WITH THE WANTINGNESS OF BEING SINGLE, AND EVEN MORE INCREASED FOR MY MOTHER'S WANTINGNESS FOR HIS LOVE IN RETURN.

"COMPASSION" IS A WONDERFUL TOOL, IT IS NOT, A DOWNFALL IN ANYONE'S LIFE. THE TRICK IS TO KNOW HOW TO USE IT EFFECTIVELY. COMPASSION OF ONE PERSON HAS THE ABILITY TO MAKE THINGS BRIGHTER IN YOUR LIFE, OR YOUR FAMILY LIFE.

"COMPASSION" IS KNOWING YOU HAVE THE ABILITY TO COMMUNICATE, EXPRESS YOUR PASSION, TOWARDS YOUR LOVED ONES.

"COMPASSION" IS THE SECOND CHANCE TO SEE YOUR LIFE MUCH BRIGHTER THAN WHAT YOU THINK OF AND SPEAK OF IT.

"COMPASSION" IS THE SECOND CHANCE TO EXPERIENCE YOUR LOVE EXPRESSED THROUGH YOU.

THIS IS WHAT OUR MOTHER'S LOVE, FOR ALL OF US IN OUR FAMILY WAS TRYING TO ACCOMPLISH. THE ACCOMPLISHMENT WAS TO KEEP US TOGETHER AS A FAMILY, TO GIVE US THAT SECOND CHANCE TO LOVE ONE ANOTHER FOR "WHO WE REALLY ARE." THIS HELPS TO EXPLAIN THE UPS AND DOWNS FAMILIES HAVE DURING THEIR RELATIONSHIPS. THE HOPE THAT THINGS

GET BETTER, THE "WISHING" FOR A LOVING FAMILY
SITUATION. THE HAPPINESS COMES BUT DOES NOT STAY
FOR VERY LONG. WHY? BECAUSE WE GIVE THANKS FOR
HAVING THIS HAPPINESS AND WHEN WE ARE THANKFUL
FOR SUCH AN ENERGY THEN IT CAN LEAVE US AT
ANYTIME. THEN THE HATE COMES BACK INTO PLAY AND
STAYS LONGER THAN THE HAPPINESS. AS THIS ROLLER
COASTER CONTINUES SOMEWHERE ALONG THE LINE
SOMEONE WILL HAVE THE CORRECT THOUGHT AND
THEN THE CORRECT SPEECH TO EITHER TURN THE
FAMILY INTO A LOVING FAMILY OR THEY WILL CREATE
A NEW WORLD, A NEW LIFE OF THEIR OWN. MOST
LIKELY IT WILL BE A NEW LIFE OF THEIR OWN WHICH
THEY WILL REACT TO BECAUSE THEY ARE UNAWARE OF
THEIR SUBCONSCIOUS CREATION, WHAT THEY ARE
AWARE OF IS THEIR ABILITY TO RUN AWAY FROM THEIR
OLD CREATION, IN TURN, CREATING A FAMILY OF THEIR
OWN, DISCONNECTING FROM THEIR PARENTS, ONLY TO
CREATE A "NEW VERSION" OF THE "OLD VERSION" OF
THEIR UNRESOLVED PAST FAMILY ISSUES. THIS IS THE
IMPORTANCE OF KNOWING HOW TO CREATE YOUR
WORLD CONSCIOUSLY. TO TAKE RESPONSIBILITY FOR
YOUR LIFE AND CHANGE IT FOR THE POSITIVE, CHANGE
IT WITH KNOWING

"YOU ARE A HIGHLY POWERFUL SPIRITUAL BEING"

AND THAT YOU CAN TEACH YOUR CHILDREN HOW TO
CREATE A LOVING FAMILY LIFE.
    LEAVING HOME AT SIXTEEN AND CREATING A NEW
WORLD FOR MY SELF, THE CHAOTIC ROLLER STILL
CONTINUED IN THE FAMILY. THINKING I HAD ESCAPED
IT, KNOWING FULLY WELL INSIDE, I HAD NOT. MY
MOTHER AND FATHER SEPARATED FOR A FEW YEARS,
THOUGH STILL SEEING EACH OTHER FROM TIME TO
TIME, THEN MY SISTER GOT MARRIED AND MOVED OUT.

A FEW YEARS LATER, MY MOTHER AND FATHER
REUNITED. THEY HAD A FUN LIFE TOGETHER FROM
TIME TO TIME, BUT IT WAS STILL A CHAOTIC ROLLER
COASTER BETWEEN THE TWO OF THEM.

THIS YO-YO EFFECT COMES FROM

"NEEDING" AND "WANTING"

THEN CHANGING OVER TO

"DESIRING" AND "WISHING"

THEN BACK TO

"NEEDING" AND "WANTING"

THEN

"DESIRING AND WISHING".

NEEDING AND WANTING PUSHES THINGS AWAY FROM
YOU.

DESIRING AND WISHING DRAWS THINGS TO YOU.

"WHAT IS THE DIFFERENCE BETWEEN NEED/WANT AND
DESIRING/WISHING?"

YOU KNOW OF WANTING AND NEEDING WHEN IT COMES
FROM THE FEELING OF PRESSURE FROM YOUR HEART
AND ON THE SIDES OF YOUR TEMPLES, THIS IS
DESPERATION, THIS PUSHES THINGS AWAY FROM YOU,
AND PLACES YOU INTO SELF-DOUBT.

WISHING AND DESIRING COMES FROM THE ENERGY

THAT SURROUNDS YOU, "YOUR ALL POSITIVE SOUL", YOU KNOW THIS FEELING BY THE WAY IT MAKES YOU FEEL. IT IS THE CONFIDENCE, THE WARM FEELING OF KNOWING THAT WHAT YOU ARE WISHING FOR, WHAT YOU ARE DESIRING IS COMING TO YOU. THIS IS WHAT "LOVE IS." THIS IS THE ENERGY THAT DRAWS THINGS TO YOU.

WHEN WANTING AND NEEDING TAKE OVER OR HAS MORE POWER THAN WISHING OR DESIRING, THE MORE THINGS ARE PUSHED AWAY FROM YOU AND THE MORE CONFLICT YOU HAVE TRYING TO OBTAIN IT AND THE MORE DESOLATION/DESPERATION A PERSON FEELS INSIDE OF THEM CREATING THAT INSTINCT FOR SURVIVAL, THE CREATION OF THE ILLUSION THAT THERE IS NOT ENOUGH TO GO AROUND, IT COINCIDES WITH BEING IN FEAR. THIS IS WHERE HOPE AND FAITH START TO LOSE THEIR POWER AND A PERSON ACTUALLY STARTS LOSING THEIR HOPE AND DESIRE AND WISHING. THEY ARE USING THEIR BRAIN AND THEIR BODY MORE AS A TOOL FOR CREATION THAN THEY ARE WITH THEIR SOUL. THIS IS WHERE THE SOUL STARTS TO SEPARATE FROM THE BODY AND THIS IS THE AGING PROCESS, THE DYING OF THE PHYSICAL BODY.

MY MOTHER NEEDED AND WANTED MORE AND MORE FOR MY FATHER'S LOVE, IN EFFECT PUSHING MY FATHER AWAY AND CREATING A HATRED INSIDE FOR HIMSELF AND FOR HER, IN EFFECT, IT CAUSED HIM TO CALL HER NAMES AND EMBARRASS HER IN PUBLIC. THE MORE MY MOTHER NEEDED AND WANTED FOR MY SISTER'S LOVE, AND MY LOVE TO MAKE UP FOR HER LOVE SHE WAS MISSING FROM MY FATHER, THE MORE WE STAYED AWAY. MY SISTER AND I DID NOT WISH TO SEE ANYMORE OF HOW OUR FATHER WAS MISTREATING OUR MOTHER. WHEN HOLIDAYS CAME AROUND MY

SISTER AND I DISLIKED THE THOUGHT OF THE FAMILY
GETTING TOGETHER. NOT KNOWING WHAT WAS GOING
TO HAPPEN, NOT KNOWING IF THEIR WOULD BE AN
ARGUMENT BECAUSE OUR FATHER WAS COMPLAINING
ABOUT SOMETHING AND THE THING WE DESPISED THE
MOST, HIS DISRESPECT FOR OUR MOTHER AND THE
BOTH OF US NOT SAYING A WORD TO HIM ABOUT IT FOR
WE WERE WISHING NOT TO CREATE A CONFRONTATION
THAT WOULD HURT OUR MOTHER AFTER WE HAD LEFT
THE GET TOGETHER. THIS WASN'T ALWAYS THE CASE,
THERE WERE GOOD FAMILY GET TOGETHERS AS WELL,
REMEMBER THE YO-YO EFFECT, THE CHAOTIC ROLLER
COASTER AND HOW ENERGY PLAYS INTO THAT. I
REMEMBER ASKING MYSELF "HOW CAN A PERSON LIVE
LIKE THAT?" THERE MUST BE A BETTER WAY.
BECAREFUL WHAT YOU ASK FOR BECAUSE YOU DO
RECEIVE THE ANSWER.

 "THE SINS OF THE FATHER ARE CARRIED ONTO THE
SON".

 THIS IS TAKEN INTO TWO CONTEXTS. IN SOME PAST
RELATIONSHIPS I STARTED ACTING LIKE MY FATHER
{MY THOUGHTS}. CONTROLLING, DOMINEERING, USING
THE FEAR OF OTHERS FOR CONTROL AND I ALSO KNEW,
THAT WASN'T THE WAY TO A HAPPY LIFE. THE SECOND
CONTEXT TO THAT PHRASE,

"THE SINS OF THE FATHER ARE CARRIED ONTO THE
SON",

"THE FIRST PART OF CREATION IS OUR THOUGHTS,"THE
FATHER",

"THE SECOND PART OF CREATION IS OUR SPEECH,"THE
SON",

WHEN YOU THINK OF A NEGATIVE SITUATION AND THEN SPEAK OF A NEGATIVE SITUATION BY ASKING FOR IT, THEN YOU WILL EXPERIENCE THAT NEGATIVE SITUATION. THEREFOR KNOW THAT SITUATION FOR WHAT IT IS, SEE THAT SITUATION FOR WHAT IT IS AND LEAVE THAT SITUATION BE AS IT IS, BE THANKFUL FOR IT THEN CREATE A MORE POSITIVE ASPECT TOWARDS YOUR LIFE. I RECEIVED MY ANSWERS THROUGH THE ACTIONS IN MY LIFE AND KNEW THAT I DID NOT WISH TO RECREATE THE FAMILY SITUATION I HAD BEEN RAISED IN. I ASKED FOR MY GUIDANCE FROM GOD, I SCREAMED IT OUT LOUD ASKING " "WHAT DO I HAVE TO DO TO BE HAPPY?",

"WHAT DO I HAVE TO DO TO MAKE THINGS RIGHT?"

 I HAVE FOUND THE ANSWERS AND I AM SHARING THEM WITH YOU,

"RIGHT NOW."

FOR WHAT I AM TO EXPRESS TO YOU NEXT MAY SHOCK YOU BECAUSE YOU WILL SEE IT FOR WHAT IT TRULY IS. THROUGH THE YEARS STILL SEEING MY FATHER VERBALLY ABUSING MY MOTHER, MY THOUGHTS WERE ON "HOW BETTER OFF SHE WOULD BE IF SHE WAS DEAD." I THOUGHT TO MYSELF, "YEAH, MY FATHER WOULD KNOW EXACTLY WHAT HE WAS MISSING IF SHE WERE GONE." OF COURSE I WOULD SPEAK OF THESE THOUGHTS TO MY FRIENDS AND FAMILY IN MY ANGERED RAGE OF HATRED FOR THE SITUATION THAT WAS OCCURRING THROUGH OUT THEIR LIFE AND MINE. MY MOTHER'S HEALTH STARTED FAILING AS WELL AS MINE. SHE HAD HER FIRST HEART ATTACK IN 1996 AND

SHE MADE IT THROUGH, BARELY. AFTER THAT EVERYTHING WENT WELL FOR ABOUT TWO YEARS. DAD TREATED HER GOOD FOR THE NEXT TWO YEARS AFTER THAT THE VERBAL ABUSE STARTED AGAIN. I STARTED SEEING LESS OF MY MOTHER AGAIN AND MY THOUGHTS TURNED TO NEGATIVITY FOR HER. HER HEALTH STARTED DETERIORATING, MY HEALTH STARTED DETERIORATING. MY SISTER'S HEALTH STARTED DETERIORATING. OUR MOTHER WANTED BOTH OF US TO COME SEE HER MORE OFTEN AND VISIT WITH HER. WITH OUR JUDGEMENTS OF OUR MOTHER'S LIFESTYLE WITH OUR FATHER AND OUR MOTHER'S WANTINGNESS FOR OUR ATTENTION, IT PUSHED US BOTH AWAY FROM HER. THE LACK OF ENERGY WE HAD TO GO VISIT AND THE FEAR OF CONFRONTATION WITH OUR FATHER AND OUR DETERIORATING HEALTH KEPT MY SISTER AND I AWAY FROM OUR MOTHER. AWAY FROM GIVING HER HOPE TO LIVE. AWAY FROM GIVING HER THE TRUE LOVE SHE DESERVED. HER DESIRE TO LEAVE HER BODY AND BE DONE WITH THIS LIFE WAS WHAT SHE TRULY SOUGHT. THERE WAS NO MORE LOVE LEFT FOR HER IN THIS LIFETIME WITH THE FAMILY SHE HAD. SHE PASSED AWAY IN 2001 FROM A MASSIVE HEART ATTACK. SHE WISHED TO CHANGE BACK INTO HER PURE POSITIVE ENERGY SO THAT SHE MAY LIVE ANOTHER LIFE IN ANOTHER TIME. I WISH THAT WHEN SHE RETURNS INTO PHYSICAL FORM THAT I MAY BE ABLE TO HELP REMIND HER OF "WHO SHE REALLY IS" AND HOW SHE CAN USE HER "BEAUTIFUL SPIRIT ESSENCE OF LOVE" TO TRANSFORM IT INTO A LOVING FAMILY, A LOVING UNIVERSE, AND HOW TO CONSCIOUSLY CREATE THIS. THREE MONTHS AFTER MY MOTHER PASSED AWAY I WENT INTO A HOSPITAL WITH THE FEELINGS OF HAVING A HEART ATTACK, MY HEART RATE WAS FINE AFTER HAVING AN EKG DONE BUT MY BLOOD PRESSURE WAS WAY TOO HIGH. THE DOCTOR ASKED ME IF ANYONE

FROM MY FAMILY RECENTLY PASSED AWAY AND I SAID YES MY MOTHER DIED THREE MONTHS AGO HIS REPLY WAS THAT HE HAD SEEN THIS HAPPEN A LOT IN HIS YEARS OF PRACTICING MEDICINE. A CLOSE RELATIVE PASSING ON AND A FEW MONTHS LATER THEY COME INTO THE HOSPITAL WITH ALMOST THE SAME SYMPTOMS AS THE RELATIVE THAT HAD PASSED AWAY. FOR SOME REASON THAT STAYED IN MY MIND AND NOW I KNOW THE ANSWER. MY JUDGEMENTS TOWARDS MY MOTHER WERE JUDGEMENTS AGAINST MYSELF. MY JUDGEMENTS TOWARDS MY FATHER WERE JUDGEMENTS AGAINST MYSELF. THE ENERGY YOU TRANSFER TO SOMEONE ELSE ALWAYS COMES BACK TO YOU. IT DIDN'T STOP THERE. A YEAR AFTER MY MOTHER PASSED AWAY, I WAS IN THE HOSPITAL BEING DIAGNOSED WITH DIVERTICULITIS. IT ALMOST TOOK ME OUT! THIS WAS CREATED BY ME, SUBCONSCIOUSLY, IN TWO WAYS. THE JUDGEMENTS TOWARDS MY MOTHER'S LIFE AND THE OTHER WAS THAT I KNEW MY HEALTH HAD BEEN DETERIORATING FOR SOMETIME AND THAT THE CAREER I WAS IN WOULDN'T LAST MUCH LONGER WITH THE WAY I WAS FEELING.

"I ASKED GOD TO KILL ME OR CURE ME"

BECAUSE I WOULD NOT LIVE LIFE THE WAY I WAS FEELING AT THAT TIME. GOD GAVE ME BOTH. BEING WEAK FROM ALL THE POISON THAT HAD ENTERED INTO MY SYSTEM, I COULD NOT MOVE, I COULD HEAR EVERYTHING. I THOUGHT TO MYSELF, "WELL THIS IS IT, 38 YEARS AND IT'S OVER, NOW WHAT?"
"THEN, I HEARD ANOTHER THOUGHT".

"IT IS UP TO YOU, IT IS YOUR CHOICE, IT HAS ALWAYS BEEN YOUR CHOICE."

HEARING THIS, BUT NOT REALLY KNOWING WHAT IT HAD DEFINED IN MY LIFE AT THE TIME, I STARTED MY RECOVERY. DOING MORE HERBAL REMEDIES AND INTERNAL CLEANSING, WATCHING WHAT I ATE AND DRANK. LEARNING MORE ABOUT THE BODY AND OUR ENVIRONMENT. THEN INTO SPIRITUALISM. THIS GAVE TO ME THE INSIGHT OF WHAT WAS HAPPENING TO ME. I WAS THE CAUSE OF IT ALL. THE NEGATIVE THINKING AND SPEAKING OF HOW MY MOTHER'S LIFE WAS BETTER OFF DEAD THAN TO LIVE IN HUMILITY FROM MY FATHER. THAT TYPE OF THINKING AND SPEAKING ACTUALLY ALMOST CREATED MY OWN DEATH OF THE BODY. IT DOESN'T HAVE TO BE A FAMILY MEMBER THAT YOU THINK ABOUT, OR SPEAK OF, IT COULD BE ANYONE OR ANYTHING. THIS THEN AGAIN IS JUDGE NOT, LESS THEE BE JUDGED! THIS WILL BRING US INTO THE COLLECTIVE CONSCIOUSNESS.

COLLECTIVE CONSCIOUSNESS

THIS IS THE SUM TOTAL OF EVERYONE'S THOUGHTS AND EVERYONE'S SPEECH. THE THING ABOUT THIS TYPE OF ENERGY IS THAT WHAT HAPPENS IS UP FOR GRABS, IF EVERYONE IS CREATING THERE WORLD SUBCONSCIOUSLY. WHAT IS DEFINED BY THIS, IS THAT ALL OF US THINK DIFFERENTLY. SOME OF US THINK POSITIVELY AND SOME OF US THINK NEGATIVELY AND THE SAME GOES FOR SPEAKING. WHAT BECOMES THE RESULT OF THIS IS THE EXPERIENCE ALL OF US WILL EXPERIENCE DEPENDING ON WHAT IS CREATED. WE ARE GIVEN EVERYTHING WE WISH TO EXPERIENCE AS INDIVIDUALS AND AS A GROUP. THIS IS WHAT IS DEFINED BY

"WAR IN THE HEAVENS."

IN A BIBLICAL SENSE, IT WAS DESIGNED TO HAVE
PEOPLE BELIEVE THAT THERE IS A WAR BETWEEN GOD
AND SATAN AND EACH IS SUPPOSED TO HAVE THEIR OWN
ARMY OF ANGELS WHOM FIGHT AGAINST ONE ANOTHER
TO SEE WHO SHALL REIGN.
   IN THE SENSE OF SENDING OUT OUR ENERGY TO THE
UNIVERSE SO THAT WE MAY EXPERIENCE "WHO WE
REALLY ARE",

"IT IS ACTUALLY A WAR BETWEEN THE POSITIVE AND
NEGATIVE THOUGHT VIBRATIONS OF EXPERIENCE".

THERE ARE THOSE THAT HAVE EXPERIENCED CERTAIN
SITUATIONS AND THOSE THAT HAVE NOT. LET'S TAKE
FOR EXAMPLE THOSE THAT HAVE EXPERIENCED THE
CLOSE UP DAMAGING EFFECTS OF A TORNADO. THEY
HAVE EXPERIENCED THE LOSS OF SUCH THINGS AS A
HOUSE, MATERIAL GOODS AND SO ON, THEREFORE THEY
KNOW OF THIS HEAVY LOSS. NOW, LET'S TAKE A LOOK
AT THOSE THAT HAVE NOT YET EXPERIENCED THIS AND
HAVE SENT THIS VIBRATION OUT INTO THE UNIVERSE.
THESE ENERGIES ARE EXACTLY THE HOT AND COLD AIR
MIXTURES IT TAKES TO FORM A TORNADO AND WHEN
THEY MEET TOGETHER IT IS ACTUALLY A WAR, A CLASH
OF CHAOS THAT CREATES DESTRUCTION, WHERE IN, NO
ONE WINS AND ALL THAT IS LEFT IS THE LOSS OF
EVERYTHING INVOLVED. NOW WHAT HAS HAPPENED IS
THE CREATION OF THE EXPERIENCE OF THE TORNADO.
THIS PHENOMENON HAS OCCURRED BECAUSE BOTH THE
POSITIVE AND NEGATIVE FORCES, THOUGHT FORMS AND
SPEECH, HAVE CREATED IT. THE THINKING AND
SPEAKING OF IT BY BOTH ENTITIES HAS BROUGHT
ABOUT IT'S CREATION. THOSE THAT HAVE ALREADY
EXPERIENCE THE EFFECTS OF A PAST TORNADO

RETHINK OF IT'S OCCURRENCE THERE FOR CREATING
THE EXISTENCE OF A NEW ONE EVEN THOUGH THEY DO
NOT WISH FOR IT TO HAPPEN AGAIN, IN THOUGHT FORM,
IT IS THEIR CASUAL SPEAKING OF THEIR EXPERIENCE OF
THE PAST TORNADO THAT BRINGS IT TO MANIFEST.
THOSE THAT HAVE NOT EXPERIENCED IT YET, THINK OF
IT AND WONDER OF THE TORNADO'S POWER AND THE
DESTRUCTION THAT CAN OCCUR FROM IT. BOTH
ENERGIES MEET AND VOILA, THEY HAVE CREATED THE
TORNADO. "WAR IN THE HEAVENS!"

IF WE WISH TO CREATE A MORE POSITIVE STYLE OF
LIFE, WE MUST START TEACHING EVERYONE HOW TO
CREATE OUR WORLDS CONSCIOUSLY. EVERYONE MUST
KNOW THAT THEY ARE A "HIGHLY POWERFUL
SPIRITUAL BEING", AND THAT WE ALL CONTROL OUR
LIVES AND THAT WITH A

"GROUP EFFORT OF POSITIVE THINKING AND
SPEAKING",

WE CAN CREATE A PARADISE FOR ALL OF US TO ENJOY
AND TO KEEP COMING BACK INTO PHYSICAL FORM TO
THIS EXOTIC PLACE THAT WE CREATE AS A GROUP. IF
ALL OF US THINK, TO CREATE AN IMAGE IN OUR
THOUGHTS, OF A BEAUTIFUL WORLD, AND ALL OF US
SPEAK OF THIS BEAUTIFUL WORLD, WE WILL
THEREFORE CREATE AND EXPERIENCE THIS WORLD AS
BEAUTIFUL. IF ALL OF US THINK OF ARMEGEDDON AND
SPEAK OF ARMEGEDDON, THEN WE WILL CREATE AND
EXPERIENCE ARMEGEDDON.

"ARMEGEDDON",

TO MANY PEOPLE, THINK IT IS THE DESTRUCTION OF
THE EARTH AND ALL LIFE IN PHYSICAL FORM.

"THIS WILL NOT HAPPEN, THIS CAN NOT HAPPEN".

"THIS WOULD MEAN TO END THE EXPERIENCE OF THE SOUL",

"TO KNOW WHAT IT IS LIKE TO FEEL AND COMPARE OURSELVES TO OTHER BEINGS".

"IT WOULD

"MEAN"

THE END OF GOD'S EXPERIENCE TO FEEL AND COMPARE OUR EXPERIENCES THAT WE GIVE TO GOD. WHAT WILL HAPPEN, IF WE DO NOT CHANGE OUR THOUGHT AND SPEECH PATTERNS FOR THE POSITIVE, IS OUR

"ADAPTATION"

TO OUR ENVIRONMENT. IN ORDER FOR LIFE TO CONTINUE IT'S EXISTENCE ON EARTH, WE HAVE AND

"ALWAYS WILL ADAPT TO OUR ENVIRONMENT".

FOR THOSE OF YOU WHO TRAVEL A LOT, YOU ALREADY KNOW THIS FEELING OF ADAPTATION, IT IS WHAT SOME PEOPLE CALL JET LAG, OR THE MOTION SICKNESS ONE FEELS IN A CAR OR BOAT. SOME EASILY ADAPT, SOME DO NOT.

"EARTH DOES NOT ADAPT TO US WE ADAPT TO THE EARTH, OR IS IT OUR ACTIONS WE ADAPT TO"?

WITH TOXIC CHEMICALS BEING MASS PRODUCED AND PLACED ONTO OUR FOOD WHILE GROWING IT, THE EARTH IS GOING TO ADAPT TO THOSE CHANGES FOR

EARTH TO SURVIVE, AND IT WILL, THEREFOR WE WILL ADAPT TO THE EARTH CHANGE AS WELL IN ORDER FOR US TO SURVIVE. IT IS A CONTINUOUS CIRCLE AND WILL FOREVER BE THAT WAY.

"THE ONE THING WE MUST KNOW OF AND REMEMBER IS", THAT IF WE WISH TO CONTINUE IN THIS LIFE FORM, THE PHYSICAL BODY AS WE NOW KNOW IT, WE MUST HELP THE EARTH CONTINUE IN IT'S BEAUTY AND LIFE. "WE ARE ALL ONE" AND THIS INCLUDES EVERYTHING,

"WHAT WE SEE AND WHAT WE DO NOT SEE".

IT IS SO APPARENT THESE DAYS WITH THE AMOUNT OF BIRTH DEFECTS INCREASING IN SIZE, THAT WE, AS A COLLECTIVE GROUP, HAVE CREATED.

"THESE ARE NOT BIRTH DEFECTS, THESE ARE "MUTATIONS" FOR SURVIVAL OF OUR NEXT GENERATIONS AND OUR NEXT GENERATIONS ARE US".

WE CAN START BY CLEANING UP OUR WATER AND STOP USING TOXIC CHEMICALS THAT POLLUTE IT AND OUR EARTH. ONCE WE BEGIN THIS EVERYTHING ELSE WILL COME TOGETHER.

"HOW ARE THESE MUTATIONS OCCURRING"?
THAT BRINGS US INTO OUR NEXT CONVERSATION ON RELATIONSHIPS.

RELATIONSHIPS

AS OUR LIFE CHANGES, SO DO OUR RELATIONSHIPS. THIS IS WHY WE CAN NOT PROMISE ANYTHING TO ANYONE.

"OUR MIND/THOUGHTS ARE ALWAYS CHANGING, THEREFOR OUR LIFE WILL CONTINUE TO CHANGE".

"WE WILL BE CONSCIOUSLY AWARE OF THIS".

WE WILL ALWAYS REMEMBER THAT EACH OF US ARE ON OUR OWN SPIRITUAL JOURNEY AND THAT WE WILL HELP NURTURE EVERYONE'S JOURNEY SO THAT IT WILL ENHANCE OUR JOURNEY. THE CELESTINE PROPHECY BY JAMES REDFIELD HAS EXPLAINED IT AS THIS.

"WE ARE A "C" LOOKING TO BECOME AN "O" SO THAT WE MAY COMPLETE OURSELVES AS A WHOLE, SO THAT ENERGY MAY BE CONTINUOUS THROUGHOUT OUR PHYSICAL LIFE",

SO WE SEARCH FOR THE OTHER HALF OF THE "C" ENERGY. WHAT WE HAVE BEEN TAUGHT IN LIFE IS TO LOOK FOR THE OTHER PARTNER TO COMPLETE THE "O", WE SEND OUT THIS ENERGY TO THE UNIVERSE WHAT WE WOULD LIKE TO HAVE AS A PARTNER IN LIFE. WHEN WE FIND THEM, EVERYTHING IN LIFE SEEMS FABULOUS, TOTAL BLISS. AS LINEAR TIME PROCEEDS ON,

"ONE STARTS TO DEMAND/TAKE MORE FROM THE

53

OTHER".

IT BECOMES A GIVE AND TAKE RELATIONSHIP IN ORDER
FOR ONE TO BECOME THE COMPLETE "O" THAT THEY
SOUGHT IN THE FIRST PLACE. IT MAY WORK FOR
AWHILE AND THE PROBLEM

"LIES WITHIN"

THAT RELATIONSHIP OF TAKING/ROBBING THE OTHER
PERSON'S ENERGY. NOTICE THAT SENTENCE,

"THE PROBLEM LIES WITHIN".

THE ROBBING OF ANOTHER'S ENERGY IS THE LIE THAT
CAUSES THE PROBLEM WITHIN THE RELATIONSHIP.
THEY ARE BOTH LYING TO THEMSELVES THAT THE ONE
GIVING ALL THE ENERGY AND THE ONE TAKING ALL
THE ENERGY DOES NOT COMPLETE EACH OTHER AS THE
COMPLETE "O". IF THEY KNEW THAT ALWAYS GIVING
TO EACH OTHER THEIR ENERGY, IN NURTURING EACH
OTHER, TO SEEK OUT DIFFERENT EXPERIENCES AND
ALLOW EACH OTHER THE ABILITY TO INDIVIDUALLY
EXPERIENCE THIS,

"THEY" {"THE" "Y" OF}

THEMSELVES WILL BECOME A COMPLETE "O" OF
ENERGY AND

"WHEN YOU COMBINE TWO COMPLETE "O"S OF ENERGY
TOGETHER IT TURNS INTO A FIGURE 8 LAYING DOWN ON
IT'S SIDE AND ANYONE THAT KNOWS OF THIS LAYING
DOWN FIGURE 8 SYMBOL, IN METAPHYSICAL TERMS, IS A
SYMBOL FOR INFINITY, NEVER ENDING, CONSTANT
FLOWING OF ENERGY, THAT CONTINUES FOREVER".

AGAIN, THIS IS THE PROOF THAT

"WE ARE ALL ONE".

 ALWAYS CONSTANT, ALWAYS LIVING, ALWAYS CHANGING OUR THOUGHTS SO THAT WE MAY EXPERIENCE OUR CREATIONS TOGETHER.

 THERE ARE MANY DIFFERENT REASONS WHY RELATIONSHIPS FAIL AND CHANGING OUR THOUGHTS ABOUT WHAT WE WISH TO EXPERIENCE, AS AN INDIVIDUAL, PLAYS A MAJOR ROLE IN THIS. SOMETIMES WE WISH TO EXPERIENCE SEX WITH ANOTHER BESIDES OUR MATE THAT WE HAVE CHOSEN, SOMETIMES IT IS LOVE, SOMETIMES IT IS WEALTH, AND SOMETIMES IT IS BEING ALONE WITH OUR THOUGHTS TO CONTEMPLATE OUR JOURNEY OF "WHY WE ARE HERE", ALONG WITH MANY DIFFERENT OTHER REASONS FOR DIFFERENT EXPERIENCES. IF YOU DESIRE MORE WEALTH AND PROSPERITY AND YOUR SPOUSE IS HAPPY WITH YOUR CURRENT WEALTH THAT YOU HAVE, THEN OF COURSE THERE WILL BE CONFLICT WITHIN THE RELATIONSHIP. YOU START WORKING MORE TO GAIN MORE WEALTH, THE SPOUSE STARTS SPENDING MORE TO RECREATE THE HAPPINESS OF THE CURRENT SITUATION THAT SPOUSE HAS COME TO ACCEPT, OF BEING CONTENT WITH YOUR CURRENT WEALTH, NOW THIS COINCIDES WITH YOU WORKING MORE TO GAIN MORE WEALTH. YOUR THOUGHTS AND SPEECH PATTERNS ARE ON WORKING MORE TO GAIN MORE WEALTH. IN YOUR MIND AND WHAT YOU HAVE BEEN TAUGHT IS THAT TO GAIN MORE YOU HAVE TO WORK MORE, SO YOUR ACTUAL GOAL IS TO WORK MORE. YOUR SPOUSES GOAL IS TO MAINTAIN THE CURRENT WEALTH THAT THEY ARE HAPPY WITH BECAUSE IT SEEMS LIKE TO THEM THAT EVERYONE IN

THE FAMILY IS HAPPY WITH THE CURRENT WEALTH, SO IN THEIR MIND THEY MUST SPEND MORE TO KEEP THE FAMILY HAPPY AND THEY ARE BECAUSE YOUR MAIN GOAL IS TO WORK MORE TO HAVE MORE, THEY ARE GIVING TO YOU EXACTLY WHAT YOU ARE DESIRING.

"THEY ARE NOT SEEKING MORE WEALTH, ONLY YOU ARE, IT IS PERFECT CREATION, WITH ALL PARTIES INVOLVED".

THE HARDER YOU WORK THE MORE THE OTHER SPOUSE SPENDS, YOU SEE THAT THERE IS NO GAIN IN YOUR HARD WORK, THEN START BLAMING YOUR SPOUSE FOR NOT HELPING YOU GAIN YOUR GOAL OF MORE WEALTH, BUT REALIZE THIS, THEY DID HELP YOU GAIN YOUR GOAL OF MORE WORK. YOU START THINKING NEGATIVELY OF YOUR SPOUSE, AS WELL AS TALKING ABOUT THEM NEGATIVELY, YOUR WORLD BECOMES FULL OF CHAOS AND YOU WONDER WHY EVERYTHING IS GOING WRONG.

"REMEMBER THIS, YOUR THOUGHTS AND SPEECH OF OTHERS ARE A REFLECTION OF WHAT YOU ARE WISHING TO EXPERIENCE FOR YOURSELF".

YOUR THOUGHTS WONDER INTO SEPARATION WITH YOUR MATE, YOU TALK OF WISHING THEY WILL MEET SOMEONE ELSE SO YOU HAVE A REASON FOR THE SEPARATION. YOUR MATE STARTS THINKING THE SAME THING THEN STARTS TALKING ABOUT IT. SOON, BOTH OF YOU ARE MEETING OTHERS AND EVENTUALLY ENDS IN A RELATIONSHIP WITH ANOTHER, THEN DIVORCE, WITH EACH OF YOU BLAMING THE OTHER FOR THE CAUSE,

"WHEN, IN ALL ACTUALITY NO ONE IS TO BLAME, IT IS LIFE RECREATED WITH NEW EXPERIENCES THAT BOTH OF YOU DESIRED, EQUAL BUT SEPARATE".

THE ENERGY OF JEALOUSY AND HATRED IN BOTH
PARTIES WERE CREATED THROUGH THE NEEDINESS AND
WANTINGNESS ENERGY OF HAVING SOMEONE TO BLAME
FOR CREATING YOUR NEW LIFE.

"THE UNIVERSAL LAW OF "LIKE ATTRACTS LIKE" IS AT
THE OPPOSITE END OF THE SPECTRUM".

"TWO FORCES WITH THE SAME MAGNITUDE BUT WITH
DIFFERENT PROPERTIES".

"WE ARE ALL ONE SEEKING DIFFERENT EXPERIENCES
THROUGHOUT LIFE".

"THE ENERGY OF NEEDINESS AND WANTINGNESS PUSHES
US AWAY FROM WHAT WE THINK TO EXPERIENCE TO
HURL US INTO THE OPPOSITE DIRECTION OF WHAT WE
DESIRE TO EXPERIENCE".

"IT IS LIKE PUTTING TWO MAGNETS TOGETHER BOTH AT
THEIR NORTH POLES, WHICH THE FORCE PUSHES THEM
AWAY, ONLY TO CONNECT THEM AT THEIR OPPOSITE
ENDS WHICH ATTRACTS, NORTH TO SOUTH".

"TO THINK OF WHAT YOU REALLY THOUGHT IS THE
OPPOSITE TO ADORN"!

HOLY TRINITY

IN THE NAME OF THE FATHER, THE SON, AND THE HOLY
GHOST

PREPARE TO LEARN THE DEFINITION FROM A DIFFERENT
TYPE OF HOST

KNOWING ALL THERE IS TO KNOW, THE FATHER CREATES
UPON US

EXPERIENCING WHAT WE KNOW, THE CLARITY IS HONEST

BEING WITH OUR TOTAL MIND GIVES TO US DESIRE

THE THREE OF THOSE COMBINED MAKES THE SPIRIT
THAT MUCH HIGHER

YOUR THOUGHTS ARE FROM A THOUGHT, FROM ANOTHER
THOUGHT WHICH FORM

TO THINK OF WHAT YOU REALLY THOUGHT IS THE
OPPOSITE TO ADORN

CONFUSING AS THAT VERSE MAY BE, IT IS A SIMPLE
PLAN

JUST CLOSE YOUR EYES AND THINK YOUR THOUGHTS,
EXPERIENCE IS AT HAND

GIVE RISE TO WHICH IS RISEN, IT TURNS TO THAT
WHICH IS

CREATE YOUR WORLD OF BEAUTY OF A NEVER ENDING
BLISS

FROM WHAT YOU LEARN OF THIS IT IS HOPED YOU
FULLY KNOW

YOUR PRESENCE ALWAYS GLOWING, ENERGY CONSTANT
FLOWING, IN A SPACE WHERE LIFE IS GRAND!

THERE ARE OTHER WAYS THAT RELATIONSHIPS END. ONE IS OF HEALTH REASONS AND THIS HAS A LOT TO DO WITH NEGATIVITY IN BOTH PARTIES. IF THE FEMALE ENERGY IS DOWN, SHE IS GOING TO ATTRACT MANY DIFFERENT TYPES OF DISEASES, AND SO WITH THE MALE. DISEASE IS CAUSED BY PARASITES AND BAD BACTERIA, WHICH WE MAINLY GET FROM EATING OUR FOODS AND DRINKING CONTAMINATED WATER. WE MUST CLEANSE OUR BODIES INTERNALLY AS WELL AS EXTERNALLY. IF THE MALE DOESN'T KEEP HIMSELF CLEAN INTERNALLY THE ENERGY FOR RELATIONSHIP WITH THE SPOUSE SHALL DETERIORATE. WITH MANY

WOMEN GETTING OVARIAN CYSTS, CERVICAL CANCER, AND TUMORS, OF COURSE THEIR GENERAL REACTION IS TO BECOME HEALTHY, THAT IS OUR SURVIVAL INSTINCT, SO

"THEY PRAY AND ASK TO BECOME HEALTHY, ASKING FOR THE ELIMINATION OF THE CAUSE OF THEIR HEALTH PROBLEMS OF OVARIAN CYSTS".

"THE UNIVERSE GIVES TO US EVERYTHING THAT WE ASK FOR CORRECTLY".

"THE ENERGY STARTS SWIRLING IN THE DIRECTION OF THE CAUSE OF THE PROBLEM WHICH IS THE HUSBAND/MATE. MOST MEN ARE SKEPTICAL OF THIS BECAUSE THEY DON'T KNOW THEY ARE PART OF THE PROBLEM".

"CHECK YOUR SEMEN MEN"!

"NOTICE IN YOUR EJACULATION OF SEMEN THE LITTLE CLUMPS OF SOFT WHITE, SOMETIMES CLEAR, CHUNKS OF MATTER. THIS IS A FUNGUS/PARASITE THAT ATTACHES ITSELF INSIDE THE FEMALE CAUSING CYSTS AND TUMORS. SOME MEN KNOW THEY ALREADY HAVE THIS BUT THINK THEY HAVE BIG SPERMS. THINK AGAIN"!

WHEN THE FEMALE IS IN PAIN AND ASKS FOR HEALING THE UNIVERSE WILL GIVE HER EXACTLY THAT. SHE WILL STOP HAVING SEX WITH THE MALE BECAUSE OF HER PAIN AND ALSO BECAUSE THE ENERGY IS BEGINNING HER HEALING PROCESS BY ELIMINATING THE SOURCE, WHICH IS THE MALE. THE MALE IS INFECTED WITH THIS FUNGUS/PARASITE AND OF COURSE THAT ENERGY IS WILLING ITSELF TO BE SPREAD OUT

AND THE MALE HAS HIS SEXUAL URGES AND SENDS OUT
THAT FREQUENCY ENERGY, HE MEETS UP WITH A
FEMALE THAT IS DESIRING WHAT IT FEELS LIKE TO
HAVE OVARIAN CYSTS AND MOST LIKELY IT IS A FRIEND
OF HIS WIFE, WHO HAS TALKED WITH HIS WIFE OF HER
EXPERIENCE SHE IS GOING THROUGH WITH OVARIAN
CYSTS/TUMORS. THE WOMEN HAVE BOTH THOUGHT IT
AND THEN SPOKE OF IT. WHICH WHAT IS LEFT IS FOR
BOTH OF THEM TO EXPERIENCE IT.

"THIS IS HAPPENING IN A SUBCONSCIOUS WAY".

THE WIFE IS ASKING FOR HEALING, WHICH IS PUSHING
AWAY THE SOURCE OF THE ILLNESS, THE HUSBAND, AND
THE HUSBAND IS SEEKING ATTENTION SEXUALLY, THE
WIFE'S FRIEND IS COMPASSIONATE TO THE BOTH OF
THEM AND HAS SUBCONSCIOUSLY ASKED FOR THE
WIFE'S EXPERIENCE AND THEN BOOM, THE
EXTRAMARITAL AFFAIR BEGINS.

"UNIVERSAL LAW "LIKE ATTRACTS LIKE" IS IN EFFECT".

THE HUSBAND AND WIFE DIVORCE, THE HUSBAND AND
GIRLFRIEND COME INTO A RELATIONSHIP, MAYBE
MARRIAGE AND IT STARTS ALL OVER AGAIN. THIS IS
ANOTHER REASON FOR BIRTH DEFECTS/MUTATIONS. IT
IS NOT ONLY THE MALES BUT WOMEN MUST KEEP
THEMSELVES CLEAN INTERNALLY AS WELL. THIS
LITTLE PARASITE/ FUNGUS, AND THERE ARE MANY
DIFFERENT TYPES, CAUSING MANY DIFFERENT
PROBLEMS.
        THIS TYPE OF ENERGY/CREATION IS HARD TO SEE
FOR SOME PEOPLE. THE BLAME IS BEING SHIFTED BACK
AND FORTH WHEN ACTUALLY THERE IS NO ONE TO
BLAME, IN TIME THE FEMALE HEALS BUT ONLY FOR
AWHILE, UNTIL SHE REFLECTS ON HER PAST

EXPERIENCE, SPEAKS OF IT TO SOMEONE, THEN SHE
MEETS ANOTHER MALE WITH THE SAME TYPE OF
FUNGUS/PARASITE HER EX-HUSBAND HAS AND SHE
BEGINS TO EXPERIENCE IT ALL OVER AGAIN. THE EX-
HUSBAND STARTS TO REFLECT ON THE PAST
EXPERIENCE OF HIS EX-WIFE AND HOW "BITCHY, SHE
WAS AND NOT GIVING HIM SEX", THEN SPEAKS OF IT TO
SOMEONE AND SOON HE MEETS SOMEONE DIFFERENT,
WHO TURNS OUT TO BE THE SAME AS HIS EX-WIFE. THIS
IS WHY THE MOST COMMON STATEMENT IS,

" I CAN SEE WHY, NOW, YOU GOT DIVORCED THE FIRST
TIME."

IT CAN BE A CONTINUOUS CYCLE IF THEY WISH IT TO BE,
IT DOESN'T HAVE TO BE THAT WAY IF YOU CAN SEE HOW
CREATION IS MADE, THINGS CAN AND DO CHANGE,

"IT IS UP TO YOU TO SEE THIS CONSCIOUSLY AND START
PRACTICING WHAT YOU ARE REMEMBERING HERE".

"YOU CREATE YOUR WORLD ACCORDING TO YOUR
WISHES, YOU CREATE YOUR WORLD ACCORDING TO
YOUR DESIRES".

"YOU REACT TO YOUR WORLD ACCORDING TO YOUR
WANTS, YOU REACT TO THE PEOPLE IN YOUR LIFE
ACCORDING TO YOUR NEEDS. WHEN YOU NEED OR WANT
THEN LIFE BECOMES A CONSTANT STRUGGLE AS WELL
AS YOUR RELATIONSHIPS".

THIS BRINGS US TO OUR OFFSPRING, WE NOT ONLY
TEACH OUR CHILDREN THE A,B,C AND 1,2,3, WE TEACH
OUR CHILDREN ABOUT LIFE AND WHAT IT IS ABOUT. IF
THEY SEE CONSTANT STRUGGLE THEN THIS IS WHAT
THEY WILL LIVE, UNLESS THEIR DESIRE IS TO SEEK A

DIFFERENT TYPE OF EXPERIENCE. WE CAN START BY
TEACHING THEM WHAT WE ARE REMEMBERING HERE
AND HOW TO UTILIZE THE TOOLS GOD HAS GIVEN US.

"THOUGHTS, SPEECH, AND EXPERIENCE".

"POSITIVE THOUGHTS PLUS POSITIVE SPEAKING EQUALS
POSITIVE EXPERIENCE. GROWTH"!

IF WE DO NOT TEACH THIS THEN THERE IS NO OTHER
CHOICE BUT TO ADAPT TO OUR ENVIRONMENT THAT WE
ARE SUBCONSCIOUSLY CREATING.

"WE ARE GOING TO HAVE TO START REACTING TO AN
ENVIRONMENT THAT IS BEING
SUBCONSCIOUSLY/UNKNOWINGLY CREATED".

LET'S GO BACK TO THE EXAMPLE OF WHY A
RELATIONSHIP ENDS DUE TO THE FEMALE HEALTH
PROBLEM. THE MALE SEMEN IS INFECTED WITH A
PARASITE/FUNGUS CAUSING OVARIAN CYSTS/TUMORS.
THE MALE BECAME INFECTED BY THE ENVIRONMENT
AND FOOD INTAKE OF HIS LIFESTYLE, OF COURSE THE
FEMALE LIVES IN THE SAME ENVIRONMENT AND MAY
OR MAY NOT HAVE THE SAME EATING HABITS. THE
FEMALE BECOMES PREGNANT AND THE COUPLE
CONTINUE TO HAVE SEX. THE MALE IS STILL INFECTED
WITH THE PARASITE/FUNGUS IN HIS SEMEN.

"THIS ALSO APPLIES TO ORAL SEX, WHAT THE MOTHER
INGESTS SO DOES THE UNBORN CHILD".

THE MUTATION/BIRTH DEFECT BEGINS AND THE CHILD
PREPARES TO ADAPT TO THE ENVIRONMENT IN WHICH
WE LIVE IN. THE CHILD MUST ADAPT IN ORDER TO
SURVIVE IN IT'S UPCOMING WORLD. THIS IS WHY IT IS SO

IMPORTANT TO KNOW HOW TO CLEAN UP OUR
ENVIRONMENT, ESPECIALLY OUR WATER SUPPLY.

"THE EARTH WILL NEVER END",

"IT CAN NOT END",

"SO, "ARMEGEDDON", AS SOME PEOPLE SEE IT WILL NOT
HAPPEN",

"WHAT CAN HAPPEN IS OUR ADAPTATION TO OUR
ENVIRONMENT".

IT IS ALSO BEST TO KNOW HOW TO KEEP CLEAN
INTERNALLY AND WATCH OUR FOOD INTAKE.

"HERBAL REMEDIES AND COLONICS CAN HELP US STAY
CLEAN INSIDE. A POSITIVE MENTAL ATTITUDE AS WELL
AS A POSITIVE FORM OF SPEECH WILL HELP US KEEP
DISEASE AND INFECTION AWAY".

THERE ARE OTHER WAYS AND REASONS WHY
RELATIONSHIPS DON'T LAST. THESE ARE A COUPLE OF
EXAMPLES OF HOW ENERGY MANIFESTS ITSELF TO GIVE
YOU WHAT YOU DESIRE TO EXPERIENCE. IF WHAT IS
GIVEN TO YOU HERE DOESN'T APPLY TO YOUR LIFE
EXPERIENCE, THEN YOU HAVE A GREAT MIND TO WORK
WITH. USE YOUR IMAGINATION AND MEMORY TO SEE
HOW THE ENERGY WORKS THAT APPLIES TO YOUR
SITUATION.

"THE BASIC TOOLS FOR CREATING YOUR LIFE.

THOUGHTS,

SPEECH, AND

EXPERIENCE/DOING.

ONCE YOU SEE HOW THESE THREE INTERACT TOGETHER YOU WILL SEE HOW YOU CAN CREATE MORE LOVE IN YOUR FAMILY LIFE AND CREATE HAPPINESS WITHIN".

MONEY

MONEY SEEMS TO PLAY AN IMPORTANT PART IN MANY PEOPLES LIVES. MONEY SEEMS TO GIVE TO PEOPLE ACCESS TO MANY DIFFERENT THINGS. PEOPLE SAY,

"MONEY CAN'T GIVE YOU HAPPINESS."

"YES IT CAN"!

"ANYTHING CAN BRING YOU HAPPINESS AS LONG AS YOU ALLOW IT TO".

THOSE THAT SAY THAT SAYING ABOUT MONEY ARE ACTUALLY PLACING A LIMITATION UPON THEMSELVES. THOUGH THEY MAY NOT BE DENYING RECEIVING MONEY, THEY ARE DENYING BEING HAPPY. IF THEY DID OBTAIN A LARGE AMOUNT OF MONEY THEN THEY WILL NOT BE HAPPY WITH IT. "

IF MONEY IS WHAT YOU DESIRE THEN ASK FOR IT, AND ASK FOR IT PROPERLY",
AGAIN NEVER NEED OR WANT IN YOUR ASKING.

"DESIRE IT",

"WISH FOR IT",

"HOPE FOR IT"

TO COME TO YOU. IT WILL MANIFEST RIGHT BEFORE YOUR VERY EYES,

"WHEN YOU STOP THINKING ABOUT IT".

WHEN YOU FIND MONEY LAYING ALONG THE ROAD, OR BASICALLY ANYWHERE, DO YOU ACTUALLY BELIEVE SOMEONE ELSE LOST IT?

"IF YOU DO THEN YOU SHOULD THINK AGAIN",

BECAUSE IF YOU DON'T THEN SOMEONE WILL COME ALONG AND SAY THEY LOST THEIR MONEY",

THEN IT WILL RECREATE IN THEIR WORLD AND NOT YOURS. THINK ABOUT THIS, IF SOMEONE DID LOSE THEIR MONEY IT ACTUALLY DEFINES THAT THEY DIDN'T DESIRE IT IN THE FIRST PLACE, AND MOST LIKELY HAD A NEEDINESS FOR IT, WHICH DEFINES THEY PUSHED IT AWAY FROM THEM BY DESIRING NOT TO HAVE IT, IF THEY CHANGE THE "NEEDINESS" BACK INTO "DESIRING" THEN IT WILL RECREATE BACK INTO THEIR LIFE, NOW IF THIS IS THE CASE AND YOU NO LONGER DESIRE THE MONEY, YOU CREATED, THAT YOU FOUND, THEN OF COURSE YOU WOULD GIVE IT BACK TO THEM, YOU YOURSELF CREATE THE NEEDINESS FOR THAT MONEY, WHICH PUSHED IT AWAY FROM YOU AND BACK TO THE ONE THAT LOST IT,
"THEREFORE MANIFESTING YOUR DESIRE FOR SAINTLINESS, INSTEAD OF MONETARY GAIN".

YOU THEREFORE CHANGED YOUR MIND ABOUT OBTAINING RICHES TO FEELING GOOD ABOUT YOUR NATURE. IT IS ALL PERFECT CREATION! YOU START THINKING YOU COULD HAVE PAID OFF A BILL WITH THAT MONEY, OR BOUGHT YOURSELF SOMETHING NICE, WHICH IS HOW YOU GOT IN THAT NEEDINESS AND WANTINGNESS MODE IN THE FIRST PLACE, WHICH MANIFESTED THE PERSON WHO SAID THEY LOST THE MONEY, THEN YOU THINK TO YOURSELF,

"IT WAS GOOD TO DO SOMETHING NICE LIKE THAT",

NOTE GIVE CLOSE ATTENTION TO THE ABOVE STATEMENT. IT WAS "GOOD" TO DO SOMETHING "NICE" "LIKE THAT". YOU ARE SAYING TO YOURSELF "YOU LIKE DOING SOMETHING NICE. THIS IS NOT A COINCIDENCE IN YOUR SPEECH PATTERN. IT IS "YOU" REMINDING "YOU" THAT YOU ARE "A PURE POSITIVE SPIRITUAL BEING", FULL OF LOVE AND KINDNESS.

 AND THAT IS DENYING THE BENEFITS OF MONETARY GAIN.
    IF YOU HAVE A CHANCE OF WORKING IN RETAIL SALES, WATCH AND STUDY THE PEOPLE THAT ARE SHOPPING OR BROWSING. LISTEN TO THEIR SPEECH. MANY TIMES YOU WILL HEAR THEM SAY,

"THIS IS NICE BUT THEY CAN'T AFFORD IT".

OR,

"THEY DON'T HAVE ENOUGH MONEY FOR IT".

EVERY TIME THEY SAY THIS THEY PUSH MONEY AWAY FROM THEM EVEN FURTHER. IF THEY WILL SAY

"I WILL BE ABLE TO AFFORD THAT SOON",

THEN THE MONEY WILL COME TO THEM TO OBTAIN
THAT ITEM. FIRST OF ALL, THEY HAVE THOUGHT ABOUT
HAVING SUCH NICE THINGS IN THEIR LIVES, THEY HAVE
SPOKEN ABOUT SUCH NICE THINGS INTO THEIR LIVES,
AND NOW THEY HAVE CREATED IT INTO THEIR LIVES BY
BEING ABLE TO SEE IT. IT IS WITHIN THEIR GRASP,
THEIR NEXT STEP WOULD BE TO THINK ABOUT THE
MONEY TO AFFORD IT, SPEAK/ASK ABOUT THE MONEY,
PROPERLY, TO AFFORD IT, THEN THEY CAN EXPERIENCE
HAVING IT IN THEIR LIFE. ONCE THEY OBTAIN
OWNERSHIP OF THAT PARTICULAR ITEM, AND
REMEMBER,

"YOU NEVER REALLY OWN ANYTHING, BECAUSE YOU
ALREADY HAVE IT",

THEN THEY CAN ENJOY THE VALUE OF IT. THE REASON
WHY MATERIAL THINGS DO NOT LAST AND
DETERIORATE THROUGHOUT TIME, IS BECAUSE THESE
ITEMS LEAVE YOUR THOUGHTS AFTER USING THEM.
WHEN YOU STARTED THINKING ABOUT WHAT IT IS YOU
WILL LIKE TO HAVE IN YOUR LIFE, TO MAKE IT
NICER/EASIER, YOU SET INTO MOTION THE CREATION OF
IT. IT STARTS TO MANIFEST THE MOMENT YOU START TO
SPEAK OF IT, THEN IT IS CREATED BRAND NEW, YOU
OBTAIN IT, USE IT, THEN START THINKING OF BETTER
THINGS, BETTER WAYS IT COULD SERVE YOUR PURPOSE.
YOU STOP THINKING ABOUT IT THEN CHANGE YOUR
MIND TO A NEWER MODEL. YOU LOSE YOUR THOUGHTS
IN MAINTAINING WHAT YOU FIRST CREATED,
THEREFORE YOUR BEGINNING CREATION STARTS TO
UNMANIFEST ITSELF BY DETERIORATING IN IT'S USE
FOR YOU. THIS APPLIES TO EVERYTHING IN YOUR LIFE.
RELATIONSHIPS, JOBS, YOUR HOUSE, YOUR CAR, YOUR

PROPERTY, ETC. ETC.

IF YOU WATCH PEOPLE COUNT THEIR PENNIES OR SEARCH FOR THE BARGAIN SALES THAT ENABLE THEM TO KEEP AS MUCH MONEY IN THEIR POCKET AS POSSIBLE, YOU WILL SEE THE TRAP THEY SET FOR THEMSELVES OF HAVING A HARD TIME BEING ABLE TO ATTRACT MORE MONEY TO THEM. THE IDEA IS TO SPEND THE MONEY YOU RECEIVE,

"SPENDING IS THE SAME AS GIVING",

THE DIFFERENCE IS WHETHER

"YOU SPEND IT HAPPILY/POSITIVELY"

OR

"SPENDING IT THINKING HARSHLY, THINKING IT AS A LOSS INSTEAD OF A GAIN".

YOU CO-CREATED THE ITEM YOU WISH TO PURCHASE BY HAVING IT AVAILABLE TO YOU, THEREFORE IT IS YOUR CREATION AS WELL, ONCE YOU PRAY FOR THE MONEY TO BE ABLE TO USE THAT ITEM IN YOUR LIFE AND RECEIVE IT, IT IS YOUR ATTITUDE ON SPENDING THAT MONEY, TO RECEIVE THAT ITEM. YOU START THINKING,

"THAT'S A LOT OF MONEY TO BE SPENDING FOR SUCH A THING, IF I GET THE LESSER VALUE ITEM, I CAN ALSO GET THIS."

WHEN DOING THIS,

YOU DENY "WHO YOU REALLY ARE."

"YOU DENIED YOUR CREATION OF THE ITEM YOU

WISHED TO HAVE",

"YOU DENIED YOUR CREATION OF THE MONEY YOU HAVE TO OBTAIN THAT FIRST ITEM".

"THIS TYPE OF ENERGY PLACES YOU IN A PATTERN OF SELF DOUBT",

"IS THIS WHAT YOU WERE REALLY SEEKING TO CREATE IN THE FIRST PLACE, SELF DOUBT"?

THIS IS SOMETHING TO BE AWARE OF CONSCIOUSLY. FOR WHEN YOU SEE THIS, YOU SEE THAT ENERGY IS CONSTANTLY FLOWING TO GIVE TO YOU THE EXACT EXPERIENCE YOU WISH TO OBTAIN. IT IS AN ENDLESS CIRCLE OF ACTION AND REACTION IF YOU SUBCONSCIOUSLY CREATE YOUR WORLD. WHEN YOU SEE AND KNOW HOW ENERGY DEFINES YOU, YOU CAN FINALLY CREATE YOUR WORLD, KNOWINGLY, AND BE IN CONTROL OF WHO AND WHAT SHALL ENTER INTO YOUR LIFE.

"YOU WILL NO LONGER BE AFRAID TO SPEND THAT MONEY, YOU CREATED",

"YOU WILL NO LONGER BE AFRAID OF ACCEPTING THAT MONEY, YOU CREATED".

"THAT'S IT"!

"YOU HAVE TO BE WILLING TO ACCEPT MORE MONEY INTO YOUR LIFE, ONCE YOU ACCEPT IT YOU WILL FREELY SPEND IT"!

SEX

IT IS THE MOST LOVING PART OF SHARING THAT WE WILL EXPERIENCE WITHIN THE HUMAN BODY. THE REASON WHY IT IS SUCH A POWERFUL DRIVE WITHIN US, PHYSICALLY AND MENTALLY, IS SIMPLY BECAUSE WE CAN NOT FEEL THIS EXPERIENCE IN PURE POSITIVE ENERGY FORM. WE CAN NOT FEEL ANYTHING WHILE IN PURE POSITIVE ENERGY FORM, WE ONLY HAVE THOUGHT IN ENERGY FORM. WE CAN GIVE OUR THOUGHTS POWER IN DIFFERENT ENERGY FREQUENCIES, BUT THAT CAN NOT BE FELT UNLESS THE BRAIN IS PRESENT TO INTERPRET WHAT THAT FEELING OF FREQUENCY WOULD BE LIKE AND WE CAN NOT HAVE A BRAIN WITHOUT A BODY TO HELP US EXPERIENCE THE MAGNITUDE OF THE EXPERIENCE WE DESIRE TO EXPERIENCE. WHEN WE ARE CHILDREN WE DON'T REALLY KNOW MUCH ABOUT SEX BUT SOME OF US HAD THE EXPERIENCE OF WALKING IN OUR PARENTS OR BABYSITTERS AND SEEING THE ACT BEING PERFORMED OR HEARING THE MOANS AND GROANS OF PLEASURABLE ECSTASY. NOW, SEEING OR HEARING THIS, OUR THOUGHTS START TO DEVELOP UPON THIS ACTION, EVEN THOUGH THE BODY HAS NOT YET REACHED THE MATURITY OF SUCH AN ACT.

"CREATION BEGINS WITH THOUGHTS",

"MANIFESTATION BEGINS WHEN THOUGHT PATTERNS MERGE WITH SPEECH PATTERNS".

A CURIOUS CHILD WITH A WILD IMAGINATION HAVE A LOT OF QUESTIONS THAT HAVE TO BE ANSWERED TO SATISFY THE REMEMBERING OF "WHO WE REALLY ARE

70

AND WHY WE ARE HERE."

"A CHILD'S THOUGHTS AND SPEECH PATTERNS, WHILE
ASKING QUESTIONS, PLAYS A MAJOR ROLE IN THE
CREATION OF MANIFESTING THEIR OWN LIFE".

THEY WILL SUBCONSCIOUSLY CREATE THEIR WORLD,
THEY WILL HAVE TO REACT TO. CHILDREN ARE
DELICATE HUMAN BEINGS, IN ORDER TO PROTECT THEM
WE WILL TEACH THEM PROPER THOUGHT IMAGES,
POSITIVE, AND PROPER, POSITIVE, SPEECH PATTERNS.

"NEVER EVER WISH YOUR CHILD TO BE GONE FROM
YOUR LIFE",

AND

"NEVER EVER TALK OF THEM AS BEING GONE EVEN IF
THEY ARE ONLY VISITING THEIR GRANDPARENTS OR
VISITING ONE OF THEIR FRIENDS".

WHEN YOU SEE HOW ENERGY OF THOUGHT AND SPEECH
COMBINE TOGETHER TO DEFINE YOU AND YOUR LIFE,
THEN YOU WILL SEE WHY THAT TYPE OF NEGATIVE
THINKING AND SPEAKING WILL BE AVOIDED.

IF YOU THINK NEGATIVELY AND SPEAK NEGATIVELY
THEN YOUR CHILDREN LEARN FROM YOU THESE
MANNERISMS AND THEY DO THE SAME THING IN
CREATING THEIR LIFE AND COMBINE THESE TWO
DIFFERENT ENTITIES WITH THE SAME TYPE OF
THINKING, BRINGS ON A COLLECTIVE CONSCIOUS
MANIFESTATION,

"WHICH IS TWICE THE POWER OF A SINGLE
INDIVIDUAL".

"CAN YOU SEE HOW NEGATIVITY CAN CREATE OUT OF THIS"?

"CAN YOU SEE, "NOW", HOW YOU WILL AVOID A HEAVY DRAMATIC SITUATION"?

"I PRAY THAT YOU DO"!

SEXUAL FANTASIES PLAY A MAJOR ROLE IN THE TYPE OF PEOPLE WE MEET THROUGHOUT OUR LIVES. MARRIED OR UNMARRIED EACH OF US EXPERIENCE SEXUAL DRIVE THROUGH SEXUAL FANTASIES. THIS IS HOW EXTRAMARITAL AFFAIRS OCCUR FOR BOTH MALE AND FEMALE.

"TEMPTATION IS BROUGHT ON TO US BY THINKING SEXUAL THOUGHTS AND SPEAKING SEXUAL DESIRES".

"THIS APPLIES IN CASUAL CONVERSATION WITH FRIENDS AND THOSE VERBAL EXPRESSIONS WE HAVE WHILE PERFORMING THE SEXUAL ACT WITH OR WITHOUT A PARTNER".

WHILE IN THE ACT OF PERFORMING SEX AND YOU CALL YOUR PARTNER BY ANOTHER NAME, YOU KNOW WHAT TYPE OF "REACTION" YOU ARE GOING TO RECEIVE FROM THEM. THEY KNOW, SUBCONSCIOUSLY, THAT YOU ARE CREATING A FUTURE AFFAIR, SEXUAL ENCOUNTER, WITH THE PERSON YOU CALLED BY NAME. YOU ARE THINKING OF THAT OTHER PERSON, YOU ARE SPEAKING THE NAME OF THE OTHER PERSON AND IT WILL MANIFEST.

"NOW, THE THING ABOUT THIS IS",

"YOU SPEAK THEIR FIRST NAME BUT NOT THEIR FULL NAME, SO IT MAY NOT MANIFEST WITH THE PERSON YOU SPOKE OF, BUT MAY MANIFEST WITH A PERSON WITH THE SAME FIRST NAME, OR MAY LOOK LIKE THE PERSON YOU THOUGHT OF AND SPOKE OF".

"NOW, LET'S LOOK AT THE PERSON YOU ARE HAVING SEX WITH AT THE MOMENT YOU CALLED THEM BY ANOTHER NAME. WHAT ARE THEY SEEKING TO EXPERIENCE"?

"IS IT THE FEELING OF THE EXPERIENCE YOU ARE GIVING TO THEM AT THAT MOMENT"?

"IS IT THAT THEY WISH FOR THEIR FREEDOM FROM THE RELATIONSHIP OF YOU, LOOKING FOR AN EXCUSE, AND NOT WISHING TO BE THE BLAME OF THE CAUSE OF THE SEPARATION"?

"POSSIBLY, ALL OF THAT".

"ONE THING FOR SURE THOUGH, IT IS ALL PERFECT CREATION"!

"I WILL NOT GO ANY FURTHER INTO NEGATIVITY OF SEXUAL ENCOUNTERS FOR I DO NOT WISH TO EXPERIENCE ANY NEGATIVITY IN MY LIFE IN THIS AREA. I WISH, I HOPE, I DESIRE, AND I WILL HAVE ALL LOVE, ALL POSITIVE ENERGY, ALL WARMTH IN ALL OF MY SEXUAL ENCOUNTERS".

"WHEN YOU GIVE LOVE YOU RECEIVE LOVE AND I APPRECIATE THIS INTO MY LIFE"!

HERE IS ANOTHER WAY FOR YOU TO LOOK UPON SEXUAL EXPRESSION. WHEN YOU HAVE SEXUAL

FANTASIES,

"IT IS THE EXPERIENCE OF ACTUALLY DESIRING TO FEEL YOURSELF",

"TO KNOW THAT YOU EXIST IN PHYSICAL FORM".

"IT IS THE ACTION OF KNOWING, YOUR {"YOU" "R"} ENERGY EXISTS WITH YOUR {"YOU" "R"} BODY AND AT THE TIME OF ORGASM YOU ARE EXPERIENCING THE SOUL AND THE BODY TOGETHER AS "ONE FORM" TRYING TO GET BACK TO BEING SEPARATE FROM EACH OTHER, AND THE SAME TO EACH OTHER.

"THIS IS WHY YOU HAVE THAT MOMENT OF GOING OUT OF YOUR MIND AND OUT OF YOUR BODY FOR A FEW BRIEF SECONDS OF TIME".

"THIS IS WHY THE BODY SHAKES AND QUIVERS AT THE MOMENT OF ORGASM".

"YOU HAVE A BRIEF MOMENT OF ONENESS WITH EVERYTHING".

"IT IS LOVE",

" IT IS BEAUTIFUL",

"IT IS PEACEFUL",

"IT IS CALMING",

"YOU BECOME PURE POSITIVE ENERGY AGAIN".

THE UP AND DOWN, THE IN AND OUT OF THE SEXUAL ACTION CREATES A HIGH VIBRATORY RATE OF INTENSE

ENERGY FREQUENCY, THAT CREATES THE SAME
FREQUENCY AS YOUR SOUL, THEREFORE ALLOWING
YOU TO BECOME UNATTACHED FROM THE PHYSICAL
BODY AT THE PEAK OF SEXUAL ORGASM. AS YOUR
FREQUENCY LOWERS IT ATTACHES ITSELF AROUND THE
BODY AGAIN, THIS IS WHY THE BODY SHAKES AND
QUIVERS.

"YOUR PURE POSITIVE ENERGY IS WRAPPING ITSELF
BACK AROUND THE BODY".

IT IS LIKE PUTTING ON A TIGHT PAIR OF PANTS. MOVING
YOUR HIPS FROM SIDE TO SIDE, SUCKING IN THE TUMMY
MUSCLES, THEN FINALLY YOU HAVE A SNUG FIT.

"AS THE SOUL WRAPS ITSELF AROUND THE BODY, IT IS
THE HIGH FREQUENCY RATE THAT SHOCKS THE LOW
FREQUENCY BODY BACK INTO PLACE".

YOU CAN ASK ALMOST ANY EMERGENCY MEDICAL
TECHNICIAN ABOUT THIS AND THEY CAN TELL YOU
ABOUT SEEING THIS EXPERIENCE IN EMERGENCIES. I
WILL NOT GO INTO FULL DETAIL OF THAT, FOR I DO NOT
WISH TO EXPERIENCE THAT TYPE OF SITUATION. YOU
CAN USE YOUR IMAGINATION ON THIS OR YOUR PAST
EXPERIENCES.

ATTRACTION

OFTEN TIMES WE VISUALIZE THE TYPE OF
SEXUAL/LOVE PARTNER WE WISH TO HAVE IN OUR LIFE.
IF YOU THINK OF PAST EXPERIENCES IN RELATIONSHIPS
AND SPEAK OF PAST EXPERIENCES IN RELATIONSHIPS,
YOU WILL CREATE THE SAME TYPE OF EXPERIENCE,

ONLY TO HAVE A DIFFERENT PARTNER TO EXPERIENCE THAT ALL OVER AGAIN.

"REMEMBER THIS",

"YOUR PAST NO LONGER EXISTS, IT SERVES YOU ONLY AS A MEMORY TO SHOW YOU HOW POWERFUL OF A SPIRITUAL BEING YOU ARE BY KNOWING AND SHOWING YOU HOW YOU CREATED IT AND TO SHOW YOU HOW YOU CAN CHANGE YOUR FUTURE FOR A MORE POSITIVE LIFE, WITHIN YOU AND WITHIN YOUR RELATIONSHIPS".

IF YOU ARE CONTINUOUSLY EXPERIENCING NEGATIVITY IN YOUR RELATIONSHIPS THEN YOU ARE THINKING AND SPEAKING OF THE NEGATIVITY IN YOUR PAST RELATIONSHIPS. THIS IS HOW JUDGEMENTS ARE FORMED IN ALL RELATIONSHIPS.

"REMEMBER, JUDGE NOT, LESS THEE BE JUDGED".

IF WOMEN THINK AND SPEAK AS ALL MEN BEING THE SAME AND MEN THINK AND SPEAK OF ALL WOMEN TO BE THE SAME, AS IN, NEGATIVE TRAITS, THEN THEY WILL CONTINUOUSLY MEET/CREATE THESE TYPES OF BEINGS INTO THEIR LIVES,

"BECAUSE WHEN YOU JUDGE PEOPLE YOU ARE ACTUALLY SAYING TO THE UNIVERSE, "THIS IS WHO YOU ARE", THIS IS WHAT YOU WISH TO EXPERIENCE AND GOD GIVES TO YOU EVERYTHING YOU ASK FOR"!

IF WOMEN THINK AND SPEAK THAT ALL MEN ARE LOOKING TO USE THEM FOR SEXUAL GRATIFICATION, THEN THIS IS THE TYPE OF MALE THEY WILL ATTRACT, AND IT IS HEIGHTENED BY THE FEMALES SEXUAL FANTASIES. THIS IS WHERE MEN GET THEIR SEXUAL

DRIVE.

"LIKE ATTRACTS LIKE".

"THE FEMALE IS WANTING AND NEEDING LOVE, WHICH IN TURN IS PUSHING LOVE AWAY, AND DESIRING TOUCH AND AFFECTION, WHICH DRAWS THE MALE TO THEM".

"THE MALE IS WANTING AND NEEDING SEX, WHICH IS PUSHING SEX AWAY, BUT DESIRING LOVE AND UNDERSTANDING, WHICH BRINGS THE FEMALE CLOSER".

"THIS IS THE TEASING PART OF RELATIONSHIPS, THE CLASH OF ENERGY BETWEEN MEN AND WOMEN".

EACH IS RECEIVING WHAT THEY DESIRE AND NOT RECEIVING WHAT THEY NEED OR WANT, BUT THEY ARE IN ALL ACTUALITY RECEIVING THEIR NEEDINESS AND WANTINGNESS AND THEREFORE RECEIVING ALL OF THEIR CREATION. IT'S A BEAUTIFUL THING WHEN YOU SEE IT FOR WHAT IT TRULY IS!

THE THING ABOUT UNDERSTANDING IS

"THAT NO ONE SHOULD UNDERSTAND ANYTHING. THE REASON BEING IS THAT WHEN YOU UNDERSTAND SOMETHING, IT DEFINES THAT YOU STAND UNDER IT. YOU ARE STATING THAT YOU ARE LESS THAN THAT".

THIS IS WHY THE WORD

"UNDERSTAND"

IS IN CONTRACTS BECAUSE THE ONES THAT INITIATE THE CONTRACTS WISH TO BE ABOVE YOU AND KNOW THIS

"THEY ARE NOT ABOVE ANYTHING, ESPECIALLY YOU!"

"ALWAYS KNOW THAT YOU HAVE THE POWER, YOU HAVE THE ABILITY TO TURN YOUR LIFE TOWARDS POSITIVITY AND HAPPINESS".

"THAT IS WHERE THE PROBLEM LIES",

THE UNDERSTANDING IS RECEIVED FOR AWHILE AND THE SOUL KNOWS IT STANDS UNDER NOTHING AND IT REGAINS IT'S STRENGTH BACK TO ONENESS. THIS APPLIES TO EVERYTHING IN LIFE, WHETHER IT IS CONTRACT OR A RELATIONSHIP.

FOR A MORE POSITIVE OUTLOOK IN SEXUALITY ALWAYS BE LOVING AND GIVE LOVE, THIS WAY NO ONE FEELS USED OR NEGLECTED.

"BE APPRECIATIVE OF THE FACT THAT YOU HAVE CREATED SUCH LOVE IN YOUR LIFE"!

APPRECIATION

LET'S TAKE A LOOK AT GRATITUDE AND WHAT THIS DEFINES TO OUR LIFE. WE HAVE BEEN TRAINED AS YOUNG CHILDREN TO SAY

"THANK YOU"

TO PEOPLE OR THINGS WHEN THEY DO SOMETHING POSITIVE FOR US IN OUR LIFE OR HELP US OUT. "WE WILL NEVER SAY "THANK YOU" AGAIN FOR POSITIVITY WHEN IT ENTERS OUR LIFE".

FOR WHEN WE SAY "THANK YOU",

"THE DEFINITION OF "THANK" IS THE PAST FORM OF THINKING AND THE FIRST LEVEL OF CREATION IS YOUR THINKING/THOUGHTS, SO IF YOU SAY "THANK YOU", YOU ARE PAST THINKING THIS POSITIVITY AND IT CAN LEAVE YOUR LIFE",

"WE WILL SAY "THANK YOU" TO NEGATIVE THOUGHTS, NEGATIVE PEOPLE, NEGATIVE ACTIONS, THIS WAY WE PAST THINK THEM, AND NEGATIVITY WILL LEAVE OUR LIFE".

"WE WILL "APPRECIATE" POSITIVE THOUGHTS, POSITIVE PEOPLE, AND POSITIVE ACTIONS SO THAT POSITIVITY WILL REMAIN/STAY WITHIN OUR LIFE",

"FOR WHEN WE "APPRECIATE" SOMETHING, WE GIVE IT "GREATER VALUE" TO DEFINING OUR LIFE AND ALLOWING POSITIVITY TO STAY WITH US",

THEREFOR

"I APPRECIATE YOU",

FOR PURCHASING AND READING THIS BOOK TO ENRICH OUR LIVES TOGETHER.

THIS WHOLE FORM OF THINKING AND SPEAKING POSITIVE IS IN THE DEFINITIONS OF WORDS THAT WE USE.

"HOW MANY OF US HAVE REALLY LOOKED AT THE WAY WE THINK AND THE WAY WE SPEAK OUR WORDS"?

"WE SPEAK OUR WORDS BY THE WAY WE WERE TRAINED TO SPEAK, NEVER REALLY GIVING CLOSE ATTENTION TO WHAT THEY ARE DEFINED AS".

"IN ALL ACTUALITY THE WORDS WE SPEAK DEFINE US AND THE EXPERIENCES THAT WE SEEK".

MANY WORDS HAVE TWO OR MORE DIFFERENT DEFINITIONS. LET'S LOOK AT THE WORD

"MEAN" OR "MEANS".

"DOES IT DEFINE THE WORD "DEFINITION" AS IN "THIS WORDS MEANS THIS"

OR IS IT "A STATE OF BEING", "A STATE OF EMOTION",

OR USED TO DEFINE A PERSON, PLACE, OR THING,

OR IS IT A "VALUE DEFINITION"?

EITHER WAY YOU LOOK AT IT, IT WILL BE ELIMINATED FROM YOUR VOCABULARY AND REPLACED WITH THE WORD "DEFINES" WHILE BRINGING POSITIVITY INTO YOUR LIFE, WHICH ALSO "DEFINES" THAT I WILL HAVE TO GO BACK INTO THIS BOOK AND CHANGE SOME WORDING AROUND. YOU SEE, I AM STILL REMEMBERING MORE KNOWLEDGE AS I WRITE THIS BOOK FOR YOU, THROUGH ME, TO YOU. THIS IS THE WAY LIFE IS, ALWAYS CHANGING AS WE REMEMBER "WHO WE REALLY ARE"! ONE THING ABOUT IT IS THAT,

"IT IS ALL PERFECT CREATION!"

NOTE HAVING GONE BACK TO THE BEGINNING OF THIS BOOK, I AM MORE AWARE OF THE POWER OF THE

WORDS THAT I CHANGED, IN GIVING A MORE CLEARER DEFINITION OF SENTENCES AND GIVING MORE POSITIVE ENERGY IN THE MESSAGE THAT IS BEING RELAYED IN HERE. THIS IS TRULY AN AMAZING KNOWLEDGE BASE TO BEGIN ONE'S LIFE TOWARD POSITIVITY, AND THE SPIRITUAL JOURNEY TO BECOMING "ONE WITH GOD", CREATING A "HEAVEN ON EARTH"!

SPEECH THERAPY

I HAVE CONSTRUCTED A GRAPH THAT HELPS TO DEFINE HOW WORDS EFFECT OUR LIFE WITH THIS ROLLER COASTER OF LIFE'S EMOTIONS. AS WE NOW KNOW, EVERYTHING HAS AN OPPOSITE.

"NEGATIVITY HAS POSITIVITY AT THE END OF IT'S SPECTRUM".

WE WILL START THERE AND CLIMB THE LADDER OF SUCCESS TOWARDS POSITIVITY. WHEN YOU SAY YOU "NEED" OR YOU "WANT" SOMETHING, WE KNOW NOW THAT YOU WILL NOT RECEIVE YOUR ULTIMATE GOAL, WHAT YOU DO RECEIVE IS THE "NEEDINESS" AND "WANTINGNESS" OF IT, WHICH IS THE FEELING OF "DESPERATION" YOU RECEIVE FOR TRYING TO OBTAIN YOUR GOAL. THE MORE YOU SAY YOU "WANT" OR "NEED" THE FURTHER IT MOVES AWAY FROM YOU. WE NOW KNOW THIS EQUALS NEGATIVITY AND "NEED" AND "WANT" IS ELIMINATED FROM OUR SPEECH.

"THE ONLY USE OF SAYING "NEED" OR "WANT" IS IN ADVERTISING, BECAUSE IN YOUR SUBCONSCIOUS IT CREATES A DESIRE WITHIN YOU TO OBTAIN THEIR PRODUCT, EVEN THOUGH YOU MAY HAVE NO USE FOR IT".

AH, NOW I KNOW WHAT YOU ARE THINKING AT THIS MOMENT. IF SAYING "NEED" OR "WANT" IS THAT EFFECTIVE IN ADVERTISING TO CREATE "DESIRE", THEN I CAN USE IT TO CREATE "DESIRE" IN MY LIFE AND RECEIVE EVERYTHING.

"NICE THOUGHT AND IT DOESN'T WORK THAT WAY"!

IT IS A TRAP FROM YOUR SUBCONSCIOUS THAT MANY PEOPLE GET THEMSELVES INTO. THIS IS WHERE THE ROLLER COASTER OF EMOTIONS COMES INTO PLAY.

"YOU OBTAIN THE "DESIRE",

"YOU OBTAIN THE PRODUCT"

"AND WHEN YOU RECEIVE IT YOUR "NEEDINESS" AND "WANTINGNESS" OF IT IS STILL THERE PUSHING IT AWAY FROM YOU AND YOU FIND THAT THE TIME AVAILABLE TO USE IT ISN'T THERE".

"IT DEFINES THAT THIS THING HAS NO DEFINITION OR VALUE IN YOUR LIFE. THIS IS WHY WE MUST ELIMINATE SAYING "NEED" OR "WANT" IN OUR SPEECH".

NOW, ONTO THE NEXT PHASE. THE WORDS

"SHOULD",

"COULD",

OR

"WOULD"

WILL BE ELIMINATED FROM OUR SPEECH AS WELL.

"THESE ARE WORDS THAT DEFINE POSSIBILITIES THAT WILL NEVER HAPPEN".

"THEY PUT YOUR LIFE "ON HOLD" AND LIFE BECOMES STAGNANT AND WHEN ENERGY BECOMES STAGNANT THERE IS NO ENERGY AT ALL THAT WILL MOVE YOUR LIFE TOWARDS POSITIVITY".

NOW, ONTO THE GREATEST OF THEM ALL. ALL OF THESE POSITIVE STATEMENTS COMING UP WILL GIVE TO YOU SUCCESS IN ALL PARTS OF YOUR LIFE. REMEMBER THESE AND PRACTICE SAYING THEM OFTEN.

"I AM"

"I WILL"

"I HAVE"

"I WISH"

"I HOPE"

"I DESIRE"

WHEN YOU BEGIN YOUR SENTENCES WITH THESE STATEMENTS YOU ARE STATING TO THE UNIVERSE/GOD,

"THIS IS WHO I AM",

"THIS IS WHAT I WISH TO EXPERIENCE".

"THESE BEGINNING STATEMENTS ARE WHAT GIVES TO YOU THE ENERGY TO BECOME WHAT YOU WISH".

"I AM" OR "I'M"

IS THE BIGGEST STRONGEST STATEMENT.

"ONCE YOU BEGIN A STATEMENT WITH "I AM" AND ADD TO IT A STATEMENT OF EMOTION {ENERGY MOTION}, YOU ARE STATING THAT YOU ARE THAT".

"THIS IS WHY YOU WILL NEVER STATE YOU ARE SORRY FOR ANYTHING".

FIRST OF ALL IT IS YOUR CREATION TO BEGIN WITH, WHATEVER THE CIRCUMSTANCE MAY BE AND SECOND OF ALL, WHEN IT IS APPROPRIATE, YOU WILL SUBSTITUTE THE WORD SORRY FOR

"APOLOGIZE".

MOST OF OUR ENGLISH LANGUAGE IS DERIVED FROM GREEK AND ROMAN TERMINOLOGY, LATIN.

"THE GREEK GOD APOLLO IS A GOD OF STRENGTH AND COURAGE AND WHEN YOU "GIZE" IT OR "IZE" IT, YOU GIVE EXTRA STRENGTH TO THE ENERGY OF MANIFESTATION".

"LIKE, REALIZE"!

THEREFORE WHEN YOU

"APOLLOGIZE"

"YOU SEND POSITIVE ENERGY OF STRENGTH AND COURAGE TO A NEGATIVE SITUATION THAT IN TURN, BRINGS POSITIVITY BACK INTO YOUR LIFE AS WELL AS

THE LIFE OF OTHERS YOU ARE SHOWING COMPASSION TO",

"YOUR "COMMUNICATION OF PASSION"!

"WHEN YOU SAY

"I WILL",

YOU ARE EXPRESSING

"YOUR FREE WILL",

"YOUR {"YOU" "R"} WILL" IS THE TORQUE, THE TWISTING TURNING MOTION OF YOUR ENERGY IN MOTION {EMOTION}, THAT IS,

"YOUR EMOTION OF MANIFESTING YOUR THOUGHTS AND SPEECH INTO MATTER",

"YOUR REALIZATION THAT IT EXISTS IN YOUR LIFE".

"I WILL",

"GIVES TO YOU THE ENERGY TO PLACE INTO MOTION YOUR ABILITY TO DO WHAT YOU SAY YOU WILL DO".

"IT IS THE DRIVING FORCE THAT ENABLES YOU".

"I HAVE" IS THE "KNOWING FORCE OF ENERGY", THAT YOU ALREADY HAVE THE ABILITY TO OBTAIN YOUR DESIRE.

"ONCE YOU KNOW THAT YOU ALREADY HAVE THIS ABILITY, BY SAYING "I HAVE", YOU AUTOMATICALLY KNOW THAT YOU "DO NOT NEED" OR "DO NOT WANT"

FOR ANYTHING BECAUSE YOU ALREADY HAVE IT".

USE YOUR POSITIVE THOUGHTS AND POSITIVE PROPER SPEECH TO MANIFEST IT IN YOUR WORLD, THEN IT BECOMES YOURS.

"I WISH" IS THE ENERGY THAT DRIVES YOUR "HOPE", WHICH DRIVES YOUR "DESIRE" FOR CREATING WHAT YOU ALREADY KNOW THAT YOU HAVE, WHICH TURNS IT INTO MATTER, WHICH GIVES TO YOU THE REALIZATION OF THE ILLUSION THAT YOU HAVE IT.

"THESE ARE SIX POWERFUL BEGINNING STATEMENTS YOU WILL UTILIZE TO CHANGE YOUR LIFE OVER TO POSITIVITY, ALL OF THE TIME"!

"I AM"

"I WILL"

"I HAVE"

"I WISH"

"I HOPE"

"I DESIRE"

ARE THE BEGINNING STATEMENTS OF PROGRESS TOWARD POSITIVITY, TO BECOMING ONE WITH GOD, WITHIN YOUR LIFE. I HAVE REPEATED THESE BECAUSE THEY ARE AN IMPORTANT PART OF YOUR LIFE.

THERE IS A LITTLE CATCH TO THESE PHRASES THAT YOU WILL BECOME AWARE OF AND IT IS CALLED

"DIVINE DICHOTOMY".

NEALE DONALD WALSCH GOES INTO GREAT DETAIL OF THIS IN HIS BOOK ON "ABUNDANCE AND RIGHT LIVELIHOOD". I APPRECIATE YOU NEALE!

DIVINE DICHOTOMY IS WHEN AT THE MOMENT YOU DECLARE YOURSELF A STATE OF BEING, YOU WILL EXPERIENCE THE OPPOSITE OF THAT STATE OF BEING YOU ARE DECLARING YOURSELF TO BE SO THAT YOU MAY KNOW YOU ALREADY ARE THAT STATE OF BEING YOU ARE DECLARING YOURSELF TO BE. NOW, THESE ARE THE MOMENTS WHEN YOUR FAITH IS BEING TESTED. THIS IS WHERE THE

"I HOPE"

"I WISH"

"I DESIRE"

COME INTO PLAY. THESE ARE FAITH STATEMENTS THAT GIVE TO YOU THE ENERGY TO OVERCOME "DIVINE DICHOTOMY." I WILL GIVE YOU AN EXAMPLE.

   WHEN I FIRST STARTED PRACTICING POSITIVE THINKING AND POSITIVE SPEAKING, AFTER READING NEALE'S "CONVERSATION WITH GOD", I STARTED THINKING OF HOW AND WHAT I CAN SAY TO DECLARE MYSELF AS. I CAME UP WITH THIS BRILLIANT, BUT NOT NEW, AFFIRMATION DECLARATION. EVERY MORNING I AWAKE FROM SLEEP, I SAY

"I AM THE HAPPINESS OF MY LIFE"
"I AM HAPPY"

AND IT DEFINES MY LIFE VERY WELL. I RECEIVED A
POSITIVE RESPONSE IN MY ATTITUDE TOWARDS MY LIFE
AND ESPECIALLY MY ATTITUDE TOWARDS PEOPLE. NOW,
I HAD READ ABOUT "DIVINE DICHOTOMY" IN NEALE'S
"CONVERSATION WITH GOD", BUT AT THE TIME DID NOT
KNOW FULLY IT'S DEFINITION. I MUST HAVE READ IT
OVER AT LEAST TEN TIMES TO TRY AND GRASP IT AND
SOON FOUND MYSELF SAYING,

"I WILL GET IT LATER."

AND I SURELY DID IN A SOURCE OF "EXPERIENCES".

HAVING THE ADVANTAGE OF ENJOYING MY
EMPLOYMENT IN RETAIL SALES, THEY CAME AS
PEOPLE/ANGELS TO THE OPPOSITE OF WHAT I HAVE
DECLARED MYSELF TO BE, AND THAT IS "TO BE HAPPY IN
MY LIFE". NOW, TO KNOW THAT "I AM HAPPY WITH MY
LIFE", I EXPERIENCED THOSE PEOPLE THAT WERE NOT
HAPPY WITH THEIR LIFE AND THEY CAME INTO THE
STORE COMPLAINING ABOUT ANYTHING. THIS STARTLED
ME IN A WAY AND HAD ME THINKING,

"HOW DID I CREATE THESE PEOPLE INTO MY LIFE?",

"HOW DID I ALLOW THEM TO BE A PART OF MY LIFE?"

I KNEW, AT THE TIME, I HAD CREATED THESE
SITUATIONS, MY NEXT QUESTION WAS

"HOW DO I AVOID THIS TYPE OF NEGATIVE ENERGY
FROM ENTERING IN MY LIFE?"

THE ANSWER CAME TO ME THE NEXT MORNING IN THE
FORM OF AN EXPRESSION,

"OTHER PEOPLE'S NEGATIVITY NO LONGER SERVES ME"

AND AS AN ADDED SPICE,

"MY NEGATIVITY NO LONGER SERVES ME!"

WHEN I SPOKE THESE COMMENTS AFTER SAYING

"I AM THE HAPPINESS OF MY LIFE"

"I AM HAPPY"

MY LIFE INSTANTLY CHANGED OVER INTO MORE
POSITIVITY THEREBY LESSENING THE EFFECTS OF
"DIVINE DICHOTOMY". I NOTICED PEOPLE WALK BY THE
STORE FRONT, LOOKING IN THE WINDOW AT PRODUCTS,
THEY WOULD STOP FOR A MOMENT THEN WALK BY. I
KNEW IT WAS NEGATIVITY WALKING BY. IT NO LONGER
IS ALLOWED TO ENTER INTO MY LIFE AND EVERYONE
THAT ENTERED INTO THE STORE IS MORE RECEPTIVE OF
ME, TO ME, AND THROUGH ME. THESE POSITIVE PEOPLE
THAT I CREATED, CREATED ME

"THE POSITIVE HAPPY, I AM"

HAVING SEEN HOW THESE POSITIVE ENERGY
STATEMENTS OF AFFIRMATION DECLARATION DEFINED
MY LIFE, I THEN ASKED FOR A CLEARER DEFINITION ON
THIS.

THE ANSWER CAME TO ME IN A FORM OF UNEXPECTED
EXPECTATION, THAT IS, KNOWING I WILL RECEIVE MY
ANSWER BUT NOT KNOWING HOW IT WILL COME TO ME
UNTIL IT PRESENTS ITSELF.
I WAS DOING AN AURA IMAGING SESSION, THAT IS,
BRINGING YOUR SOUL TO VISUALIZATION, SO THAT YOU

MAY SEE HOW YOUR THOUGHTS EFFECT YOUR LIFE, UPON A CLIENT.

SHE HAD A BOOK BY NEALE DONALD WALSCH, "ABUNDANCE AND RIGHT LIVELIHOOD", KNOWING THAT I AM A BIG FAN OF NEALE'S WRITINGS, SHE PRESENTED IT TO ME. AS I READ THE PART ABOUT "DIVINE DICHOTOMY", I INSTANTLY KNEW THE DEFINITION OF IT AND KNEW, AUTOMATICALLY, WHY I DID NOT FULLY KNOW OF IT WHEN I READ IT THE FIRST TIME.

"I HAD TO HAVE THE EXPERIENCE OF "DIVINE DICHOTOMY"

TO FULLY GRASPS ITS DEFINITION AND TO TAKE IT A BIT FURTHER SO THAT I MAY EXPRESS THIS TO YOU RIGHT HERE AND RIGHT NOW.

 "YOUR THOUGHTS ARE FROM A THOUGHT FROM ANOTHER THOUGHT WHICH FORM TO THINK OF WHAT YOU REALLY THOUGHT IS THE OPPOSITE TO ADORN."

THIS IS "DIVINE DICHOTOMY", AND THE TOOLS {WORDS} TO GET PAST THE OPPOSITE OF WHAT YOU DECLARE YOURSELF TO BE IS THE FAITH THAT YOU HOLD IN YOUR POSITIVE THOUGHTS AND POSITIVE SPEAKING OF

"I WISH"

"I HOPE"

"I DESIRE"

BECAUSE THE PERSISTENCE OF YOUR FAITH WILL GIVE TO YOU THE ULTIMATE HAPPINESS YOU ARE DECLARING YOURSELF TO BE. YOU WILL THEN MEET MORE

POSITIVE PEOPLE THAT ACCEPT "WHO YOU REALLY ARE" AND MOST IMPORTANTLY, "YOU" WILL ACCEPT "WHO YOU REALLY ARE", AND THAT IS ANYTHING AND EVERYTHING YOU DECLARE YOURSELF TO BE!

OK INTELLIGENT PEOPLE, I KNOW WHAT YOU ARE THINKING BECAUSE MY THOUGHTS WENT THERE AS WELL AND I AM THANKFUL OF THOSE THOUGHTS. SO, RETHINK YOURSELF BACK TO POSITIVITY AND KEEP THE FAITH. YOU KNOW WHO YOU ARE AND IT IS YOUR SOUL SETTING YOURSELF UP. THIS IS THE SOUL'S JOB AND THE REASON WHY IT IS DOING WHAT IT IS DOING IS SO THAT YOU MAY KNOW IT CONSCIOUSLY AND REMEMBER THAT YOU ARE "A HIGHLY POWERFUL, HIGHLY POSITIVE SPIRITUAL BEING"!

KNOWING YOUR SOUL

BY THE WAY, LET'S ANALYZE THAT WORD COMPLAIN FOR A BIT. WHEN SOMEONE IS COMPLAINING TO YOU, THEY ARE

"COMMUNICATING THEIR PLAINESS"

TO YOU AND WITH THE KNOWLEDGE YOU HAVE REMEMBERED THIS FAR, YOU ARE MORE THAN JUST PLAIN AND SO ARE THEY. IT IS UP TO YOU HOW YOU HANDLE THEIR COMPLAINING. YOU CAN CHOOSE TO JOIN THEM IN THEIR PLAINESS OR YOU CAN USE THAT OPPORTUNITY TO PRESENT TO THEM, AND YOURSELF, THE POSITIVITY YOU NOW KNOW YOU WILL ALWAYS HAVE, AND REMEMBER IF SOMEONE COMES INTO YOUR LIFE COMPLAINING, KNOW THAT YOU CREATED THEM IN YOUR LIFE, OTHERWISE, THEY DO NOT EXIST, OR PRESENT THEMSELVES TO YOU IN YOUR PRESENCE.

91

LET'S EXAMINE ALSO THE WORD "THEIR", WHICH IS TO DEFINE A SECOND OR THIRD PARTY, WHICH IS A

"JUDGEMENT WORD"

FOR YOU ARE USING THIS IN A WAY TO TALK OF SOMEONE ELSE, AND ALSO DEFINING

"THE"

"I"

"R"

OF YOU. AS IN

"I R THIS"

AND

"I R THAT".

WHEN YOU THINK AND SPEAK OF SOMEONE YOU ARE IN ALL ESSENCE THINKING AND SPEAKING OF YOURSELF, YOU ARE CREATING YOUR WORLD, AND WHAT YOU WISH TO EXPERIENCE, THIS IS

"THE I R OF YOU".

OK, LET'S GET TO KNOWING YOUR SOUL AND WHAT IT WISHES TO EXPERIENCE, BECAUSE AFTER ALL, IT IS "WHO YOU REALLY ARE", AND YOUR SOUL RECEIVES EVERYTHING IT DESIRES TO EXPERIENCE. AS I STATED EARLIER, YOU CAN PROPHESIZE YOUR OWN FUTURE BY LISTENING TO WHAT YOU ARE SAYING TO OTHERS IN

CASUAL CONVERSATION. YOU CAN ALSO PROPHESIZE YOUR OWN FUTURE BY LISTENING TO WHAT OTHERS ARE SAYING AS WELL. YOU WILL KNOW,

"BY LISTENING TO WHAT THEY ARE SAYING",

"WHAT THEY ARE WISHING TO EXPERIENCE",

"BY HOW THEY ARE SAYING THEIR SENTENCES".

THE KEY WORDS TO LOOK FOR WHEN THEY ARE SPEAKING ARE

"I AM"

"I WILL"

"I HAVE"

"I WISH"

"I HOPE"

"I DESIRE"

WHEN THEY ARE USING THESE KEY WORD PHRASES IN A POSITIVE MANNER OF SPEAKING YOU WILL KNOW IN AN INSTANT, THESE ARE POSITIVE PEOPLE TO BE AROUND AND ALLOW THEM TO ENTER INTO YOUR LIFE. THIS WILL LEAD YOU INTO PROGRESS OF YOUR LIFE TOWARDS POSITIVITY.

IF THEY ARE USING THESE KEYWORD PHRASES IN A NEGATIVE WAY, YOU WILL INSTANTLY KNOW TO GIVE THEM POSITIVE ENERGY AND THEN SEND THEM ON THEIR WAY TO RETHINK THEIR LIFE ANEW.

WHEN YOU HEAR A PERSON SAY

"I AM WILLING TO DO THIS"

OR

"I WILL HAVE THIS READY FOR YOU",

THEY ARE GIVING TO THEMSELVES THE ENERGY TO BRING UP THEIR ABILITY TO DO WHAT THEY ARE WILLING THEMSELVES TO DO.

IF THEY ARE SAYING

"NEED"

"WANT'

"SHOULD"

"COULD"

"WOULD"

IN ANY OF THEIR SENTENCES THEN YOU INSTANTLY KNOW WHERE THERE ENERGY IS AND THEIR ABILITY TO DO THAT REMAINS AS IT IS

"ABLE TO DO IT"

WE ARE ALL ABLE TO DO EVERYTHING AND ANYTHING,

THE QUESTION IS "ARE WE WILLING OUR ENERGY TO ACTIVATE OUR ABILITY TO DO ANYTHING AND EVERYTHING"?

"THIS KNOWLEDGE IS WHAT DEFINES A GREAT LEADER, A GREAT MASTER, AND A GREAT STUDENT".

SEEING THE ENERGY AND HOW IT EFFECTS THEM AND THE LIVES OF OTHERS.
"THIS KNOWLEDGE ENCOURAGES US TO MAKE THE CORRECT DECISIONS IN DEFINING OUR LIFE".

IN ANOTHER ESSENCE OF CREATING YOUR WORLD, IT IS NOT WHAT THEY ARE SAYING TO YOU THAT GIVES POSITIVE ENERGY INTO YOUR LIFE, IT IS YOUR RESPONSE, IN SPEECH, OF WHAT THEY ARE SPEAKING OF TO YOU, THAT GIVES TO YOU AND THEM THE POSITIVE ENERGY.

AFTER ALL, YOU HAVE CREATED THIS BEING YOU ARE SPEAKING TO, YOU HAVE ALLOWED THEM TO ENTER INTO YOUR LIFE. THEY ALREADY EXIST IN THE BIG WORLD THAT DOES NOT "MATTER" IN YOUR WORLD.

WHAT "MATTERS" IN YOUR WORLD IS TO KNOW THAT YOU CREATED THEM, ALLOWED THEM TO "MATTER" IN YOUR WORLD WHEN YOU SPEAK WITH THEM.

"WHAT IS "MATTER" DEFINED AS"?

MATTER IS THE JOINING OF ATOMIC AND SUBATOMIC PARTICLES TO CREATE INTO "BEING" A SUBSTANCE OF WHICH YOU CAN FEEL AND EXPERIENCE SO THAT YOU CAN COMPARE YOURSELF TO THIS AND TO KNOW THAT YOU EXIST, DIFFERENT TO IT, BUT OF THE SAME TO IT AND WHEN YOU SEE THIS, YOU KNOW THEN THAT "WE ARE ALL ONE".
THIS APPLIES ALSO TO FEELINGS OF EMOTION, NOT ONLY TO MATERIAL OBJECTS, BECAUSE IT IS ALL

ENERGY, WE ARE ALL ENERGY. TAKE A LOOK AROUND YOU WHEN YOU ARE IN A PUBLIC PLACE. ALL OF THE PEOPLE AROUND YOU EXIST IN YOUR LIFE BUT DO THEY MATTER IN YOUR LIFE? THEY DO AND THEY DON'T. YOU ARE ABLE TO COMPARE YOURSELF TO THEM, NOW I AM SAYING COMPARE YOURSELF TO THEM,

"DO NOT JUDGE THEM".

AS YOU LOOK AT PEOPLE AROUND YOU, YOUR THOUGHTS ARE BEGINNING YOUR CREATION,

"THOUGHTS" BEING THE FIRST LEVEL OF CREATION ARE VERY ETHEREAL, LIGHT ENERGY, AND WHAT IS THOUGHT OF BUT NEVER SPOKEN CREATES ONLY UPON THE FIRST LEVEL OF CREATION.

"IT DOESN'T MATTER"!

"GET IT"?

NOW, WHAT DOES MATTER IS THE MOMENT YOU BEGIN TO SPEAK WITH SOMEONE, BECAUSE WHEN YOU SPEAK YOUR WORDS, IT IS THE DENSEST PART OF ENERGY THAT BEGINS YOUR CREATION, IT IS AS YOU NOW KNOW THE SECOND LEVEL OF CREATION,

THIS IS WHEN ENERGY TURNS INTO MATTER, THEREFORE WHAT MATTERS IN YOUR LIFE IS,

"WHAT YOU ARE THINKING",

"HOW YOU ARE THINKING",

"WHAT YOU ARE SPEAKING",

"AND HOW YOU ARE SPEAKING IT"!

 WHEN YOU OBSERVE THIS CONSCIOUSLY/KNOWINGLY,
YOU WILL KNOW WHAT YOUR SOUL IS DESIRING TO
EXPERIENCE AND IF IT IS AN EXPERIENCE YOU HAVE
ALREADY EXPERIENCED AND DO NOT WISH TO
EXPERIENCE IT AGAIN, WHETHER YOU LIKED IT OR
DISLIKED IT, THEN YOU CAN CONSCIOUSLY/KNOWINGLY
CHANGE IT, THEREBY BRINGING YOUR SUBCONSCIOUS
SOUL INWARD TO YOUR CONSCIOUS/KNOWING AND
HAVE COMPLETE CONTROL OF YOUR WORLD.

"THIS IS GOING WITHIN INSTEAD OF GOING WITHOUT"!

ALSO KNOW THAT THE PERSON YOU ARE SPEAKING
WITH MATTERS IN YOUR LIFE BECAUSE YOU HAVE
CRYSTALLIZED THEM INTO YOUR PRESENCE, WHICH
GIVES TO YOU THE OPPORTUNITY TO CREATE YOU,
YOUR LIFE, AND THE ENERGY OF MATTER THAT YOU
WISH TO EXPERIENCE.

NOW, REMEMBER THIS,

"ENERGY OF MATTER",

FOR IT IS ALSO

"A STATE OF BEING",

"A STATE OF FEELING, AS IN A FEELING OF LOVE, A
FEELING OF BEING IN GREAT OPTIMAL HEALTH, A
FEELING OF POSITIVE ENERGY".

"I THINK YOU WILL GET THE PICTURE".
   YOU MAY BE ASKING,

"WHY DOES MY SOUL SET ME UP TO EXPERIENCE NEGATIVE FEELINGS OR SITUATIONS?"

IT IS A VERY SIMPLE ANSWER.

"YOU CAN NOT KNOW WHAT POSITIVITY IS UNLESS YOU KNOW THE OPPOSITE END OF THE SPECTRUM, WHICH IS NEGATIVITY".

NOW, YOU ALREADY KNOW WHAT NEGATIVITY IS AND THAT IT NO LONGER SERVES YOU. BE "THANKFUL" FOR IT AND SEND IT BACK INTO THE UNIVERSE WITH YOUR LOVE AND GOD'S BLESSING

AND START "NOW" TO APPRECIATE POSITIVITY, BECAUSE AS PURE POSITIVE ENERGY, WE ARE ALL "POSITIVE" AND THIS IS "WHO WE REALLY ARE", "PURE POSITIVE ENERGY", AND THE ONLY WAY WE CAN TRULY KNOW THAT WE EXIST AS "PURE POSITIVE ENERGY", IS TO EXPERIENCE THE OTHER END OF THE SPECTRUM, WHICH IS NEGATIVITY IN PHYSICAL BEING.

THE UP AND DOWN EMOTIONAL ROLLER COASTER OF LIFE,

THROW IN A COUPLE OF LOOPS OF DIVINE DICHOTOMY

AND IT BECOMES AN AMAZING RIDE!

ALMOST THERE ALWAYS KNOWING, ALWAYS POWERFUL AGAIN AND THEN THE LOSS OF FAITH TO GIVE YOU THAT EXTRA SURGE FOR THE DOWN HAUL AND THEN BACK UP AGAIN.

NOW, WITH THE KNOWLEDGE YOU KNOW AND THE INTELLIGENCE TO USE THAT KNOWLEDGE YOU WILL

CREATE "HEAVEN ON EARTH", ALWAYS A HIGHLY POSITIVE, HIGHLY POWERFUL SPIRITUAL BEING IN HUMAN BEING FORM. PEACE ON EARTH, GOOD WILL TO ALL!

"THIS IS OUR GOAL HERE IN PHYSICAL FORM",

"TO FEEL OUR EXISTENCE",

"BY WAY OF EXPERIENCE",

"TO RE-MEMBER",

"THAT WE ARE",

"AS PURE ENERGY",

"ALL POSITIVE",

"ALL LOVE",

"ALL CREATIVE",

"AND ALL KNOWING"!

ABILITY WORDS

LET'S LOOK AT THE ABILITY OF THE WORD "CAN", AS IN,

"I CAN DO THIS".

OF COURSE YOU CAN, YOU SEE, YOU ALREADY KNOW YOU HAVE THE ABILITY TO DO EVERYTHING. WHAT YOU

SEEK IS THE ENERGY TO PUT FORTH YOUR ABILITY INTO ACTION.

THIS IS WHERE

"I WILL"

COMES INTO PLAY. THAT WORD

"WILL"

GIVES TO YOU THAT ENERGY TO PUT INTO MOTION YOUR ABILITY TO DO WHAT YOU SAY YOU WILL DO. TAKE OUT THE WORD

"CAN"

FROM YOUR VOCABULARY BECAUSE, AFTER ALL,

"WHAT IT DOES IS PUTS YOUR ENERGY IN A CAN AND STORES IT".

YOU DON'T HAVE TO STORE ENERGY ONCE YOU KNOW YOU ARE ABUNDANT IN ENERGY AND IT IS ALWAYS FLOWING, ALWAYS GIVING TO YOU IN IT'S NATURE.

YOU HAVE THE ABILITY TO BE ANYTHING AND EVERYTHING YOU WISH TO BE. IT IS HOW YOU THINK OF IT AND HOW YOU SPEAK OF IT THAT MANIFESTS INTO YOUR BEING.

"HOW YOU PLACE YOURSELF INTO MOTION TO BECOME WHAT YOU DESIRE TO BE IS THE APPLICATION OF INTELLIGENCE OF THE KNOWLEDGE YOU HAVE REMEMBERED HERE AND THROUGHOUT YOUR ENTIRE LIFE".

"BE KNOWING OF THE THOUGHTS YOU THINK THAT ARE DEFINING YOU",

"BE KNOWING OF THE WORDS YOU SPEAK AND WRITE TO OTHERS AND THEIR {THE}{I}{R} DEFINITIONS OF THOSE WORDS,"

THAT ARE, IN ALL ACTUALITY, DEFINING "WHO YOU ARE" AND "WHAT YOU WISH TO EXPERIENCE".

"WHEN YOU START GIVING ATTENTION TO YOUR THOUGHTS AND YOUR WORDS, YOU START GIVING ATTENTION TO {YOU}{R}{SELF}",

THEN THIS TURNS ITSELF INWARD TO GIVE YOU INTENTION OF CREATING YOU, YOUR LIFE {YOU}{R}{LIFE}, KNOWINGLY/CONSCIOUSLY. THIS IS ALSO GOING WITHIN YOUR {YOU}{R} SOUL INSTEAD OF GOING WITHOUT YOUR SOUL. BRINGING YOUR UNCONSCIOUS TO YOUR CONSCIOUS, THEREBY BECOMING

"ONE"

WITH GOD!
   AS YOU START TO THINK POSITIVE THOUGHTS AND SPEAK POSITIVE WORDS TO AND OF OTHERS, WATCH THE POSITIVE CHANGE IN THE PEOPLE AROUND YOU AND HOW THEY REACT TO YOU. SEE THAT I WROTE

"REACT"

BECAUSE WHEN PEOPLE CREATE THEIR WORLD SUBCONSCIOUSLY/NOT KNOWINGLY THEN THEY "REACT" TO THEIR ENVIRONMENT AND PEOPLE THAT

ENTER THEIR LIVES, THEREFORE THEY WILL "REACT" TO YOU, IN OTHER WORDS, THAT ARE DEFINING "REACT" THEY WILL GIVE TO YOU AND THEMSELVES,

"ANOTHER PERFORMANCE"

OF "WHO THEY ARE" AND "WHAT THEY WISH TO EXPERIENCE", AND IF THEY ARE NEGATIVE IN THEIR THOUGHTS AND WORDS AND IF YOU ARE UNAWARE OF THIS, YOU MAY

"PERFORM AGAIN"

WHAT THEY ARE BRINGING TO YOU. THIS IS YOUR "ALL POSITIVE" SOUL SETTING YOURSELF UP TO EXPERIENCE A NEGATIVE SITUATION SO THAT IT MAY EXPERIENCE ITSELF AS THE OPPOSITE OF WHAT YOU TRULY ARE AND THAT IS THE

 "ALL POSITIVE YOU"

THIS IS WHY IT IS SO IMPORTANT TO BE CONSCIOUSLY AWARE OF YOUR THOUGHTS AND THE WORDS YOU SPEAK AND WRITE. NOW, WE WILL, WITH POSITIVE THOUGHTS AND POSITIVE SPEECH CHANGE TO A NEW POSITIVE

"SCENE"

"SEEN"

"SEEING"

AND BECOME THE DIRECTOR OF THE PERFORMANCE OF POSITIVITY IN OUR CONTROL OF THE DIRECTION AND IN CONTROL OF THE ACTORS/ACTRESSES THAT ARE

NOTICING
WATCHING THE CHANGE OVER
TO POSITIVITY

THIS IS SOMETHING, AS I WRITE THIS BOOK TO YOU, THROUGH ME, I AM STILL GAINING KNOWLEDGE IN WORDS THAT I AM WRITING. LET'S TAKE

"NOTICE"

"NOTICING"

AND SEPARATE IT. "NOT ICE", "NOT ICING". WHAT DOES IT DEFINE? A NON-SLIPPERY SURFACE? WET BUT NOT COLD ENOUGH TO FREEZE? NOT PUTTING A TOPPING ON A CAKE? OR IS IT

"NO TICING"?

TO ENTICE SOMEONE OR SOMETHING IS TO GET THEIR DESIRE BUILT UP, WHICH IN TURN BUILDS UP THEIR CURIOSITY, WHICH BUILDS UP THEIR ENERGY FOR THEM TO PERFORM A CERTAIN TASK TO OBTAIN THE KNOWLEDGE OF THE USE OF WHAT YOU ARE ENTICING THEM TO RECEIVE. THEREFORE "NO TICING" IS NOT A WORD WE WILL USE IN THIS CIRCUMSTANCE. THIS IS WHY I KEPT IT PRESENT IN THE ABOVE CAPTION AND SWITCHED IT OVER TO "WATCHING". I WISH TO ENTICE YOU TO WATCH THE CHANGE OVER INTO POSITIVITY, BE AWARE OF HOW THE ENERGY MANIFESTS INTO YOUR LIFE AND BE AWARE OF THE POWER YOU HAVE OVER

THE PEOPLE THAT ENTER INTO YOUR LIFE. AS I STATED
EARLIER OF MY FIRST PRACTICING OF POSITIVITY WITH
THE DECLARATION OF

"I AM THE HAPPINESS OF MY LIFE"

AND THE EXPERIENCES OF DIVINE DICHOTOMY THAT
CAME WITH THAT AND OF COURSE THE AFFIRMATION
DECLARATION OF

"OTHER PEOPLE'S NEGATIVITY NO LONGER SERVES ME",

THAT FOLLOWED WHICH LESSENED THE SEVERITY OF
DIVINE DICHOTOMY, YOU WILL SEE THE CHANGE IN
PEOPLE AROUND YOU OF ENTERING POSITIVITY.

"KNOW THIS AND KNOW IT WELL",

YOU DO NOT HAVE TO SEEK THE PEOPLE OF POSITIVITY,
THEY WILL FIND YOU",

AFTER ALL, YOU HAVE CREATED THEM.

"WATCH FOR THEM IN THEIR SPEECH AND
MANNERISMS".

THESE ARE PEOPLE THAT ARE DEFINED BY YOU, THAT IS
"DEFINING YOU", BECAUSE WHAT YOU SAY TO THEM
YOU ARE SPEAKING ABOUT YOU AND WHAT YOU WISH
TO EXPERIENCE.

"YOUR WORDS WILL EFFECT THEM AND THE GREATEST
EFFECT OF YOUR SPOKEN WORDS EFFECT YOU MORE".

"YOU RECEIVE WHAT YOU GIVE"!

"WILL YOU SEE THIS"!

"I WILL YOU TO KNOW THIS"!

WHEN ATTEMPTING TO HELP SOMEONE, YOU ARE IN ALL ACTUALITY ATTEMPTING TO HELP YOURSELF. IF THEY ARE NOT RECEPTIVE OF YOUR ATTEMPT TO HELP THEM, YOU ARE, IN ALL ACTUALITY, NOT RECEPTIVE IN ATTEMPTING TO HELP YOURSELF. THIS IS WHEN YOU SHALL CONTEMPLATE ON THE SITUATION AT HAND AND ASK,

"HOW DID I CREATE THIS"?

IS IT THE STATE OF BEING "REJECTED" WHAT YOU ARE LOOKING FOR? IS IT THE STATE OF BEING OF

"SELF DOUBT",

THAT YOU SOUGHT AND RECEIVED. KNOW THIS AS

"REFLECTION".

"KNOW THIS AND KNOW IT WELL",

THEY HAVE ALSO CREATED THEIR WORLD AND ARE BASKING IN THEIR "PERFECT SUBCONSCIOUS CREATION OF REACTION".

IT IS THEIRS AND YOU CAN NOT TAKE IT AWAY FROM THEM "NO MATTER" HOW HARD YOU TRY.

IT IS UP TO THEM TO ASK THE QUESTION FOR POSITIVE CHANGE AND ONCE THEY ASK, IT IS STILL UP TO THEM TO LISTEN FOR THE ANSWER AND THEY ALREADY ASKED, THIS IS WHY YOU ARE IN THEIR LIFE AND THEY

ARE IN YOURS.

"CO-CREATION".

IF THIS HAPPENS TO YOU BE "THANKFUL" FOR THOSE EXPERIENCES AND BE "APPRECIATIVE" OF YOURSELF FOR THE KNOWING OF THE CONSCIOUSNESS OF AWARENESS THAT IS BEING BROUGHT TO YOUR ATTENTION, RIGHT NOW! THIS IS THE KNOWING OF THE CHANGE OVER TO POSITIVITY.
YOU AND YOU ALONE ARE RESPONSIBLE IN CREATING YOUR LIFE BY THE THOUGHTS THAT YOU THINK AND THE WORDS THAT YOU SPEAK. IN OTHER WORDS

"YOU AND YOU"

"ALL ONE"

ARE

"RESPONSE ABLE"

IN CREATING YOUR LIFE BY THE THOUGHTS THAT YOU THINK AND THE WORDS THAT YOU SPEAK".

"RESPONSIBLE",

"RESPONSE ABLE",

"IS, THE ENERGY OF THE ACTION YOU GIVE TO YOUR SELF BY THE THOUGHTS YOU THINK AND THE WORDS YOU SPEAK. "I WILL"!

ALLOW US, NOW, TO SEE THE WORD "RECREATION"

AND THE DEFINITION THAT IT HOLDS. DOES IT REALLY DEFINE RELAXATION OR HAVING FUN OR DOES IT DEFINE

"RE CREATING YOU R LIFE A NEW"?

HOW ABOUT THE WORD

"CREATURES"?

IS IT ACTUALLY

"CREATE YOURS", "CREATE YOU R"

OR DOES IT DEFINE ANIMAL BEINGS THAT YOU CREATE? HOW ABOUT THE WORD

"EXAMINE"?

DOES IT DEFINE "TO LOOK AT", "TAKE INTO CONSIDERATION", A PART OF "YOU R LIFE"? THESE ARE WORDS THAT ARE WORTH YOUR ATTENTION, TO THINK OF AND TO SPEAK OF IN A POSITIVE WAY TO BRING YOU, CREATE YOU, A PARADISE, A BEAUTIFUL HAPPY LIFE.

"BE/A/U/THAT/IS/FULL OF LIFE".

WOW, THIS IS POWERFUL STUFF TO KNOW. I AM EXCITED IN BEING, BEING ABLE TO SHARE THIS WITH YOU. LET US LOOK AT THE WORD "DESIRE". WHAT DOES IT DEFINE?

"DESIRE"

"DE" IS SPANISH, AND ALSO FRENCH, I BELIEVE, AS "OF" OR "OF THE". "SIRE" IS OLD OR MIDDLE ENGLISH DEFINING

"FATHER"

AND IS MOSTLY DEFINING AS THE FATHER OF DOMESTICATED ANIMALS. IN ANY TERM, "FATHER" IS EQUAL TO OUR THOUGHT/THINKING WHICH IS ALSO EQUAL TO GOD.

"IT IS THE FIRST LEVEL OF CREATION".

THEREFORE WHEN YOU SAY

"I DESIRE"

YOU ARE PLACING INTO MOTION THE ENERGY OF

"I, OF FATHER",

"I, OF GOD",

"I, OF THOUGHTS,"

"I, OF MY THOUGHTS,"

THE "YOU" OF YOUR "THINKING", THEREBY YOU BECOME "WHAT YOU ARE THINKING" AND YOU EXPERIENCE WHAT YOU ARE SAYING YOU ARE DESIRING,

"THE FATHERING THOUGHT"!

"I WILL YOU TO SEE THIS IN A MOST WONDROUS LIGHT"!

I HAD AN INTERESTING CONVERSATION THE OTHER DAY, WHERE I WAS EXPRESSING MY THOUGHTS AND SPEECH TO A PERSON ABOUT TAKING THE WORDS "NEED" AND "WANT" OUT OF THE VOCABULARY OF OUR SPEECH. SHE EXPRESSED TO ME THAT THE WORDS

"NEED" AND "WANT" SERVE HER IN A POSITIVE WAY
ACCORDING TO THE VIBRATORY EFFECTS OF HER
VOCALIZATION OF HER SPEECH.

IN OTHER WORDS,

"HOW SHE USES THEM" IN A POSITIVE WAY".
AS I LISTENED TO HER ,INTENTLY, SHE FOLLOWED IT UP
WITH, "I AM LOOKING FORWARD TO SEEING YOU ATTEND
THE "RETREAT". THIS WAS OUR INITIAL CONVERSATION
OF AN EVENT THAT WAS TO TAKE PLACE. AS I EXPRESSED
TO HER THE SPEECH THERAPY I HAVE WRITTEN ABOUT
IN THIS BOOK ABOUT NEEDING AND WANTING AND THE
ROLE IT PLAYS IN OUR SPEECH,

SHE REPLIED,

"THEN WE CAN AGREE TO DISAGREE."

THIS STOPPED OUR CONVERSATION. BOTH OF OUR
THOUGHTS CEASED TO BE EXPRESSED THROUGH
VOCALIZATION OF SPEECH. WE EXPRESSED OUR
GREATFUL NATURE FOR EACH OTHER IN A POSITIVE
MANNER AND HUNG UP THE PHONE. AS I SAT THERE
CONTEMPLATING THE NATURE OF OUR CONVERSATION
AND HOW I CREATED THIS PERSON AND THE MESSAGE
THAT WAS GIVEN TO ME AND WHAT I HAD GIVEN TO HER,
AS A MESSAGE. IT DAWNED ON ME THAT SHE HAD GIVEN
ME A SALES PRESENTATION TO PURCHASE A TICKET TO
ATTEND THE EVENT WE WERE TALKING ABOUT.

THEREBY, THE WORDS "NEED" AND "WANT" SERVE HER
POSITIVELY IN ADVERTISING TO CREATE A DESIRE
WITHIN OTHERS TO PURCHASE TICKETS TO AN EVENT
THAT WILL CREATE A FINANCIAL GAIN IN HER LIFE.

NOW, THERE IS NOTHING, "NO" "THING", WRONG WITH THAT. WHY? BECAUSE

"THERE IS NOTHING WRONG NOR IS IT RIGHT THERE IS ONLY EXPERIENCE".

WHAT IT DOES DO THOUGH IS CREATE THE DESIRE WITHIN YOU TO PURCHASE TICKETS TO THE EVENT, BUT WILL THE MESSAGE OF THE EVENT SERVE YOU?

"WILL IT STAY WITHIN YOU TO DEFINE YOU"?

LIKE I STATED EARLIER IN THIS BOOK ABOUT NEEDING AND WANTING IN ADVERTISING, IT IS VERY EFFECTIVE IN CREATING DESIRE WITHIN YOU TO OBTAIN THE PRODUCT, TO PERFORM A CERTAIN TASK, TO OBTAIN THE USE OF THE PRODUCT AND USE IT FOR A SHORT PERIOD OF TIME, BUT THEN LATER ON YOU HAVE NO USE FOR IT,

"THEREBY IT IS NOT A PROGRESSIVE STEP FORWARD TOWARDS YOUR POSITIVE LIFE".

IT, AT BEST, PLACES YOUR LIFE ON HOLD OR CREATES YOUR LIFE IN A NEGATIVE SETTING CAUSING YOU TO LIVE YOUR LIFE BACKWARD. THIS IS WHY THINGS DO NOT LAST FOREVER IN LIFE, WHEN IN ALL ACTUALITY THEY CAN LAST FOREVER IN YOUR LIFE, WHEN YOU DESIRE TO THINK POSITIVELY AND SPEAK POSITIVELY. THEREFORE, WE WILL REMOVE THE WORDS "NEED" AND "WANT" FROM OUR VOCABULARY OF SPEECH AND REPLACE THEM WITH

"I AM"
"I WILL"

"I HAVE"

"I WISH"

"I HOPE"

"I DESIRE"

THEREFOR GIVING TO US POSITIVE ENERGY TO PROGRESS INTO A POSITIVE LIFE, BECOMING "ONE" WITH GOD.

"I AM THANKFUL FOR THE NEGATIVE THOUGHTS AND THE NEGATIVE WORDS I HAVE WRITTEN HERE TODAY, THEY SERVE ONLY AS A TOOL IN "REMEMBERING HOW POWERFUL, HOW POSITIVE OF A SPIRITUAL BEING" WE TRULY ARE, AND I APPRECIATE ALL POSITIVITY IN MY THOUGHTS AND SPEECH TO PROGRESS US INTO A LOVING WORLD FOR EACH OTHER".

THE STATEMENT SHE EXPRESSED,

"WE AGREE TO DISAGREE",

IS A VERY EFFECTIVE AND POWERFUL STATEMENT, AS IN,

"IT CREATED, IN THE BOTH OF US, A WEB OF PEACE AND TRANQUILITY IN OUR MINDS/THOUGHTS".

"IT IS VERY USEFUL IN A WAY TO PREVENT ANYTHING YOU SEE AS NEGATIVE FROM ENTERING INTO YOUR LIFE".

"IT IS A STATEMENT OF LAYING DOWN A LEVELING FIELD BETWEEN TWO EGOS".

"IT IS PROCRASTINATION ON THE PART OF THE ONE WHO

SAYS IT".

"WHAT IS PROCRASTINATION"?

"PROCRASTINATION IS THE LEVELING FIELD OF THE EGO. WHAT WOULD HAPPEN TO YOU IF YOU WERE "RIGHT" ALL THE TIME? THERE WILL BE NO MORE ROOM FOR SELF-DOUBT AND IF THERE IS NO ROOM FOR SELF-DOUBT THEN YOU WILL BE "ALL KNOWING", "ALL POWERFUL" AND THIS IS WHAT YOU TRULY ARE, "ALL KNOWING", "ALL POWERFUL", "A HIGHLY POSITIVE", "HIGHLY POWERFUL SPIRITUAL BEING, WRAPPED AROUND A HUMAN BEING FORM OF ENERGY".

"REMEMBER, THERE IS NO RIGHT, THERE IS NO WRONG, THERE IS ONLY EXPERIENCE".

 THEREFORE I HAVE COME TO THE REALIZATION OF OUR MESSAGES TO EACH OTHER.

MY MESSAGE WAS FOR HER TO TAKE THE WORDS "NEED" AND "WANT" OUT OF HER THOUGHTS AND SPEECH AND REPLACE THEM WITH

"I AM"

"I WILL"

"I HAVE"

"I WISH"

"I HOPE"
"I DESIRE"

SO THAT SHE MAY PROGRESS HER LIFE INTO POSITIVITY

AND TO ADVANCE HER SPIRITUAL ESSENCE INTO THE "ALL KNOWING" AND TO BE AWARE OF HER SELF-DOUBT. BE THANKFUL OF IT AND APPRECIATE HER LIFE INTO THE "ALL KNOWING". FOR THE QUESTION SHE HAS ASKED OF GOD AND THE UNIVERSE IS FOR MORE TRUTH AND LIGHT. SHE HAS BEEN GIVEN HER ANSWER THROUGH OUR CONVERSATION ON THE PHONE.

HER MESSAGE TO ME IS THAT, "I AM ALL KNOWING","ALL POSITIVE" AND TO PROGRESS INTO POSITIVITY BY RELAYING THIS MESSAGE TO YOU, RIGHT NOW, IN THIS BOOK, SO THAT YOU MAY GRASP THE ESSENCES OF YOUR MESSAGES IN CASUAL CONVERSATION WITH OTHERS. I SEE NOW THE POWER OF STATEMENTS AND THE POWER OF WORDS IN STATEMENTS THAT GIVE TO US THE ENERGY TO PROGRESS INTO POSITIVITY.

"THE ALL KNOWING"

I WILL THAT YOU SEE THIS, I WILL THAT YOU ARE HAPPY WITH THIS KNOWLEDGE.

SOME PEOPLE HAVE BROUGHT MY ATTENTION TO THE AFFIRMATION DECLARATION OF

"MY NEGATIVITY NO LONGER SERVES ME"

I AM THANKFUL OF NEGATIVITY IN MY THOUGHTS, AS IN, I PAST THINK IT, FOR IT HAS SERVED ME ONLY TO KNOW OF HOW I CREATED IT IN MY PAST LIFE EXPERIENCES. I CLAIM OWNERSHIP OF IT SO THAT I MAY CHANGE IT INTO POSITIVITY. THIS GIVES TO ME THE APPRECIATION {UPLIFT} OF MY SELF TO ENTER INTO POSITIVITY. AS PURE ENERGY, WE ARE ALL POSITIVE, ALL LOVING, THEREFORE TO KNOW THAT WE ARE POSITIVE WE MUST EXPERIENCE THE OPPOSITE END OF THE SPECTRUM,

WHICH IS NEGATIVITY, THIS IS US BEING IN HUMAN FORM, THIS IS US AS HUMAN BEINGS. TO EXPERIENCE NEGATIVITY TO BRING US BACK TO POSITIVITY TO TRULY KNOW THAT WE ARE ALL POSITIVE. THIS IS WHY OUR SOUL SETS US UP AND DRAWS TO US THE TYPE OF PEOPLE WE SPEAK WITH IN CASUAL CONVERSATIONS. THE SOUL KNOWS IT IS ALL POSITIVE, ALL LOVING, ALL CREATING, WHAT THE SOUL DOESN'T KNOW IS THE EXPERIENCE OF IT, THEREFORE CREATING THE OPPOSITE END OF THE SPECTRUM TO FULLY EXPERIENCE THE POSITIVENESS OF IT'S SELF, OUR SELF, IN HUMAN BEING FORM. WHEN WE REALIZE THIS WE CAN THEN CREATE A REAL "HEAVEN ON EARTH".

PRAYER

LET US GIVE CLOSE ATTENTION TO THIS WORD. WHAT DOES THIS WORD DEFINE? IS IT TO MEDITATE {THINK} ABOUT YOUR LIFE? IS IT TO ASK GOD TO FOR GIVE YOU THE ENERGY {THE WILL} FOR POSITIVE THINGS IN YOUR LIFE AND THE LIFE OF OTHER'S? ARE YOU ASKING GOD TO FORGIVE YOU FOR NEGATIVE THINKING, NEGATIVE SPEAKING, AND NEGATIVE ACTION? FORGIVENESS IS NOT ABOUT EXCUSING YOU OR SOMEONE FOR NEGATIVE THOUGHTS, NEGATIVE SPEECH, AND NEGATIVE ACTION. FORGIVENESS IS

"FOR"

"GIVING"
YOU THE ENERGY {YOUR WILL} TO OVERCOME THOSE NEGATIVE THOUGHTS, SPEECH, AND ACTIONS. FORGIVENESS IS

"FOR"

"GIVING"

YOU THE ENERGY {YOUR WILL} FOR POSITIVE
THOUGHTS, POSITIVE SPEECH, AND POSITIVE ACTIONS.
THEREFOR, DO NOT FORGIVE NEGATIVITY, BE THANKFUL
FOR NEGATIVITY, SO THAT YOU MAY PAST THINK IT AND
NEGATIVITY WILL LEAVE YOUR LIFE. FOR GIVE OF
POSITIVITY, "FOR" WHEN YOU ARE "GIVING" POSITIVE
THOUGHTS, POSITIVE SPEECH, AND POSITIVE ACTION
YOU ARE "FOR GIVING" POSITIVITY TO YOURSELF AND
ALL THOSE THAT ENTER INTO YOUR LIFE. LET US
CONTINUE WITH THE WORD "PRAY" AND ALSO "PREY"
THESE ARE TWO WORDS WITH DIFFERENT SPELLING AND
OF THE SAME DEFINITION.

"PRAY", TO SEEK.

"PREY", TO HUNT.

THESE ARE ACTION WORDS THAT DEFINE ENERGY IN
MOTION AND ENERGY IS IN MOTION CONSTANTLY.
EVERY TIME YOU THINK, EVERY TIME YOU SPEAK, YOU
ARE PRAYING. YOU ARE SETTING INTO MOTION YOUR
ENERGY TO MANIFEST EXPERIENCES IN YOUR LIFE.
   THE LORD'S PRAYER IS A VERY POWERFUL AND
USEFUL PRAYER TO MEDITATE UPON AND TO SPEAK OF
AND TO PUT INTO USE. LET'S GIVE THIS PRAYER MORE
ATTENTION AND DEFINE IT WORD FOR WORD.

THE LORD'S PRAYER

OUR FATHER, WHO ART IN HEAVEN

HALLOWED BE THY NAME
THY KINGDOM COME
THY WILL BE DONE
ON EARTH AS IT IS IN HEAVEN
GIVE US THIS DAY OUR DAILY BREAD
AND FORGIVE US OUR TRESPASSES
AS WE FORGIVE THOSE WHO HAVE TRESPASSED
AGAINST US
AND LEAD US NOT INTO TEMPTATION
BUT DELIVER US FROM EVIL
FOR THINE IS THE POWER AND THE GLORY
IN THE KINGDOM
FOREVER AND EVER
AMEN!

"OUR" = OF OR RELATING TO US OR OUR SELF, ESPECIALLY AS POSSESSORS OR POSSESSOR OF AN ACTION. GROUP, THE HOLY TRINITY.

"FATHER" = A MAN WHO HAS BEGOTTEN A CHILD, ONE THAT ORIGINATES OR INITIATES. ALSO THE FATHER IS EQUAL TO GOD WHICH IS EQUAL TO OUR THOUGHTS, WHICH IS THE FIRST LEVEL OF CREATION.

"WHO" = AS ONE THAT

"ART" =   THE CONSCIOUS/KNOWING USE OF SKILL AND CREATIVE IMAGINATION.

"IN" =   FUNCTION WORD TO INDICATE PURPOSE.

"HEAVEN" = A PLACE OR A CONDITION OF UTMOST HAPPINESS. {PURE POSITIVE ENERGY}

"HALLOWED" = TO MAKE HOLY. {TO MAKE WHOLE}

"BE" = TO EQUAL IN DEFINITION, TO HAVE IDENTITY WITH.

"THY" = POSSESSOR OR AGENT, OBJECT OF AN ACTION.

"NAME" = A WORD OR SYMBOL USED TO DESIGNATE AN ENTITY. ENTITY IS THE ENERGY YOU CREATE. ENTITY IS "BEING"/ "EXISTENCE". "IN THE NAME OF" = "BY AUTHORITY OF."

"THY" = POSSESSOR OR AGENT/OBJECT OF AN ACTION.

"KINGDOM" = A REALM OR REGION IN WHICH SOMETHING IS DOMINANT.

"COME" = TO REACH A CONDITION.

"THY" = POSSESSOR OR AGENT/OBJECT OF AN ACTION.

"WILL" = USED TO EXPRESS A COMMAND, DETERMINATION, INSISTENCE, PERSISTENCE.

"BE" = TO HAVE IDENTITY WITH, TO HAVE, MAINTAIN, OR OCCUPY A PLACE, SITUATION, OR POSITION.

"DONE" = TO BRING TO PASS, TO PUT FORTH.

"ON" = USED AS A FUNCTION WORD TO INDICATE POSITION IN CONTACT WITH AN OUTER SURFACE. "EARTH" = THE SPHERE OF MORTAL LIFE AS DISTINGUISHED FROM SPHERES OF SPIRIT LIFE.

"AS" = TO THE SAME DEGREE OR AMOUNT, {COMPARING}.

"IT" = EXPRESSES A CONDITION OR ACTION WITHOUT REFERENCE TO AN AGENT.

"IS" = TO EQUAL IN DEFINITION, TO HAVE IDENTITY WITH.

"IN" = USED AS A FUNCTION WORD TO INDICATE PURPOSE.

"HEAVEN" = A PLACE OR CONDITION OF UTMOST HAPPINESS. {PURE POSITIVE ENERGY}

"GIVE" = TO MAKE PRESENT "PRE" "SENT" OF

"US" = GROUP, I WILL DEFINE THIS AS THE HOLY TRINITY,{THE FATHER, THE SON, AND THE HOLY SPIRIT}{YOUR THOUGHTS, YOUR WORDS, YOUR ACTION/EXPERIENCE.}

"THIS" = THE PERSON, THING, OR IDEA THAT IS PRESENT {WHAT YOU ARE ASKING FOR TO CREATE} OR NEAR IN PLACE, TIME, OR THOUGHT OR THAT HAS JUST BEEN MENTIONED.

"DAY" = THE TIME OF LIGHT BETWEEN ONE NIGHT AND THE NEXT. { THIS IS INTERESTING BECAUSE CREATION COMES TO YOU AT THE SPEED OF LIGHT, THAT IS 186,000 MILES PER SECOND. I WILL SHOW YOU LATER HOW YOU WILL KNOW THIS IS TRUE.

"OUR" = OF OR RELATING TO US AS POSSESSORS OF AN ACTION. THE HOLY TRINITY.

"DAILY" = OCCURRING, MADE, OR ACTED UPON EVERYDAY.

"BREAD" = A USUALLY BAKED OR LEAVENED FOOD MADE OF A "MIXTURE" WHOSE BASIC CONSTITUENTS IS FLOUR OR MEAL. "THE MIXTURE OF THE HOLY TRINITY."

"AND" = USED AS A FUNCTION WORD TO EXPRESS LOGICAL MODIFICATION AND CONSEQUENCE ALSO TO JOIN ONE FINITE VERB TO ANOTHER SO THAT TOGETHER THEY ARE LOGICALLY EQUIVALENT TO AN INFINITIVE PURPOSE.

"FORGIVE" = TO GIVE UP RESENTMENT OF OR REQUITTAL. FOR GIVING OF ENERGY TO.

"US" = GROUP, "THE HOLY TRINITY."

"OUR" = POSSESSORS OF AN ACTION {POWER}

"TRESPASSES" = AS A DICTIONARY DEFINITION IT IS DEFINED AS TREADING UPON ANOTHER'S TERRITORY WITHOUT PERMISSION. IF WE SEPARATE THIS WORD, "TRES", IS SPANISH FOR THREE, WHICH DEFINES THE HOLY TRINITY. "PASSES" = TO SERVE AS A MEDIUM OF EXCHANGE, TO BE ACCEPTED OR REGARDED. TO IDENTIFY ONES SELF OR BE IDENTIFIED AS ONE IS NOT.

"AS" = TO THE SAME DEGREE OR AMOUNT, COMPARING.

"WE" = GROUP, "THE HOLY TRINITY".

"FORGIVE" = FOR GIVING ENERGY TO.

"THOSE" = THE ONE NEARER OR MORE IMMEDIATELY UNDER OBSERVATION OR DISCUSSION.

"WHO" = AS ONE THAT.

"HAVE" = TO ACQUIRE OR GET POSSESSION OF, TO CAUSE OR COMMAND TO DO SOMETHING, TO CAUSE TO BE IN A CERTAIN PLACE OR STATE.

"TRESPASSED" = "HOLY TRINITY" = "TRES" "PASSED" = THE THREE, TO MOVE IN A PATH SO AS TO APPROACH AND CONTINUE BEYOND SOMETHING.

"AGAINST" = COMPARED OR CONTRASTED WITH.

"US" = GROUP, "THE HOLY TRINITY".

"AND" = EQUIVALENT TO AN INFINITIVE PURPOSE.

"LEAD" = TO GUIDE ON A WAY, ESPECIALLY BY GOING IN ADVANCE TO DIRECT ON A COURSE OR IN A DIRECTION TO SERVE AS A CHANNEL FOR.

"US" = GROUP, "THE HOLY TRINITY."

"NOT" = USED AS A FUNCTION WORD TO STAND FOR THE NEGATIVE OF A PRECEDING GROUP OF WORDS.

"INTO" = IN THE DIRECTION OF, TO THE STATE, CONDITION, OR FORM OF.

"TEMPTATION" = TO RISK THE DANGERS OF, TO INDUCE TO DO SOMETHING, TO CAUSE TO BE STRONGLY INCLINED.

"BUT" = EXCEPT FOR THE FACT, WITH THE EXCEPTION OF.

"DELIVER" = TO SET FREE, TO TAKE AND HAND OVER TO, TO ASSIST IN GIVING BIRTH.

"US" = GROUP, "THE HOLY TRINITY."

"FROM" = USED AS A FUNCTION WORD TO INDICATE PHYSICAL SEPARATION OR AN ACT OR CONDITION OF REMOVAL, ALSO TO INDICATE THE SOURCE CAUSE OR BASIS OF.

"EVIL" = THE FACT OF SUFFERING, MISFORTUNE, AND WRONGDOING, A COSMIC EVIL FORCE. SOMETHING THAT BRINGS STRESS, SORROW, OR CALAMITY.

"FOR" = USED AS A FUNCTION WORD TO INDICATE PURPOSE OR TO INDICATE THE RECIPIENT OF A PERCEPTION, DESIRE, OR ACTIVITY.

"THINE" = THAT WHICH BELONGS TO THEE.

"IS" = TO HAVE IDENTITY WITH, TO HAVE AN OBJECTIVE EXISTENCE, HAVE REALITY OR ACTUALITY.

"THE" = USED AS A FUNCTION WORD TO INDICATE THAT A FOLLOWING NOUN OR NOUN EQUIVALENT IS DEFINITE OR HAS BEEN PREVIOUSLY SPECIFIED BY CONTEXT OR BY CIRCUMSTANCE.

"POWER" = ABILITY TO ACT OR PRODUCE AN EFFECT, POSSESSION OF CONTROL, AUTHORITY, OR INFLUENCE OVER OTHERS.

"AND" = EQUIVALENT TO AN INFINITIVE PURPOSE.

"THE" = FUNCTION WORD TO INDICATE DEFINITE.

"GLORY" = PRAISE, HONOR, OR DISTINCTION EXTENDED BY COMMON CONSENT {UNIVERSAL LAW, LIKE ATTRACTS LIKE.} A DISTINGUISHED QUALITY OR ASSET.

"IN" = USED AS A FUNCTION WORD TO INDICATE PURPOSE.

"THE" = FUNCTION WORD TO INDICATE DEFINITE.

"KINGDOM" = A REALM OR REGION IN WHICH SOMETHING IS DOMINANT.

"FOREVER" = FOR A LIMITLESS TIME, AT ALL TIMES.

"AND" = EQUIVALENT TO AN INFINITIVE PURPOSE.

"EVER" = AT ANY TIME, IN ANY WAY.

"AMEN" = USED TO EXPRESS SOLEMN RATIFICATION OR HEARTY APPROVAL. EXPRESSION OF FAITH.

IN WORDS THAT ARE DEFINING "THE LORD'S PRAYER"

MY THOUGHTS, WHICH ORIGINATE FROM ONE THAT IS CONSCIOUSLY/KNOWINGLY THE USE OF MY SKILL OF CREATIVE IMAGINATION TO INDICATE MY PURPOSE OF BEING TO CREATE FROM A CONDITION OF UTMOST

HAPPINESS {PURE POSITIVE ENERGY}

MAKE WHOLE THAT WHICH I CREATE INTO BEING SO THAT I MAY EXPERIENCE THIS TO KNOW "WHO I REALLY AM."

I, THE POSSESSOR OF POWER TO CREATE THIS REGION TO REACH A CONDITION OF KNOWING "WHO I REALLY AM."

I, THE POSSESSOR OF POWER, COMMAND TO HAVE IDENTITY WITH, BY COMPARING MYSELF TO MY CREATIONS, PUT FORTH THIS CREATION AND BRING IT TO PASS SO THAT I MAY EXPERIENCE "WHO I REALLY AM."

BRING FORTH MY CREATION TO MY MORTAL LIFE TO THE SAME DEGREE THAT I AM ASKING TO COMPARE MYSELF TO AND EXPRESS THIS CONDITION OR ACTION THAT IS EQUAL TO DEFINING MY IDENTITY WITH MY

PURPOSE OF BEING AND THAT IS A
CONDITION OF UTMOST
HAPPINESS, WHICH IS PURE
POSITIVE ENERGY.

MAKE PRESENT THIS CREATION
TO THE HOLY TRINITY, WHICH IS
OUR THOUGHTS, OUR WORDS, AND
OUR EXPERIENCE THAT HAS BEEN
MENTIONED AND MAKE MANIFEST
THROUGH THE TIME OF LIGHT AS
POSSESSORS OF POWER SO THAT
WE MAY KNOW OF OUR POWER AND
BE REMINDED OF THIS EVERYDAY
TO KNOW THAT OUR THOUGHTS,
OUR WORDS, AND ACTIONS OF OUR
EXPERIENCE DEFINE "WHO WE
REALLY ARE."

MAKE THIS CREATION KNOWN
TO ME SO THAT I MAY EQUAL THIS
TO MY INFINITE PURPOSE FOR
GIVING OF MY ENERGY TO THE
WHOLE THREE OF THAT I AM, THE
THOUGHTS, THE WORDS, AND THE
EXPERIENCE FOR WHICH I AM THE

POSSESSOR OF POWER THAT
TURNS THE THREE INTO THE
POWER OF ONE SO THAT THIS
CREATION MAY SERVE AS A
MEDIUM OF EXCHANGE SO THAT I
MAY CHOSE TO ACCEPT OR
REJECT THIS EXPERIENCE AS TO
"WHO I REALLY AM."

TO COMPARE THIS CREATION,
WHICH MY THOUGHTS, MY WORDS,
AND MY EXPERIENCE/ACTION HAS
GIVEN ENERGY TO, SO THAT I MAY
OBSERVE AND COMPARE MYSELF
AS ONE, THAT I ACQUIRED
THROUGH MY COMMAND TO CAUSE
TO BE IN CREATION BY MY
THOUGHTS, MY WORDS, AND MY
EXPERIENCE/ACTIONS TO MOVE IN
A PATH SO AS TO APPROACH AND
CONTINUE BEYOND MY SPIRITUAL
JOURNEY THAT I HAVE COMPARED
MY SELF AND MY POWER AS ONE
CREATED BY THE HOLY TRINITY OF
ME, WHICH IS MY THOUGHTS, MY

WORDS, AND MY EXPERIENCE/ACTION, SO THAT I MAY FULLY KNOW "WHO I REALLY AM."

MAKE THIS CREATION EQUAL TO MY INFINITE PURPOSE, TO GUIDE ME, TO DIRECT ME, TO SERVE AS A CHANNEL FOR MY ONENESS WITH GOD, BY WAY OF MY THOUGHTS, MY WORDS, AND MY EXPERIENCE/ACTION, IF THIS CREATION IS IN THE DIRECTION OF NEGATIVITY OR TO RISK THE DANGERS OF LIFE, THEN MANIFEST MY CREATION WITH THE EXCEPTION OF THE DANGER TO LIFE AND TO SET FREE BY ASSISTING IN GIVING BIRTH TO MY CREATION THROUGH MY THOUGHTS, MY WORDS, AND MY EXPERIENCE/ACTION, THE PHYSICAL SEPARATION OF THE ACT OR CONDITION OF REMOVAL OF ANY SUFFERING, MISFORTUNE,

OR WRONGDOING.

MY CREATION GIVES TO ME MY
PURPOSE OF BEING SO THAT I MAY
PERCEIVE THAT WHICH BELONGS
TO ME, TO HAVE IDENTITY WITH
MY PURPOSE OF BEING, THAT IS
DEFINED BY MY DISTINGUISHED
QUALITY TO INDICATE MY
DEFINITE PURPOSE, IN A WORLD
WHICH I DOMINATE AT ALL TIMES
WITH MY INFINITE PURPOSE, AT
ANY TIME, IN ANY WAY, WITH MY
EXPRESSION OF FAITH AND
HEARTY APPROVAL!

NOW, KNOWING OF THIS KNOWLEDGE THAT HAS BEEN
GIVEN UNTO YOU, YOU HAVE TO ADMIT THIS IS VERY
POWERFUL AND VERY USEFUL INFORMATION. THE
LORD'S PRAYER IS A COMMAND, A PROTECTOR, AND A
MESSAGE ALL IN ONE. IT IS A COMMAND THAT BRINGS
FORTH YOUR CREATION SO THAT YOU CAN EXPERIENCE
THE POWER THAT YOU HOLD "WITHIN" YOU, BY
COMBINING THE HOLY TRINITY TO MAKE MANIFEST
YOUR EXPERIENCES SO THAT YOU HAVE SOMETHING TO
COMPARE YOURSELF TO AND TO "KNOW" YOU. IT IS
ALSO PROTECTING YOU FROM ANY HARM BY YOUR
CREATION, EITHER TO YOU OR BY YOU, THAT WOULD
ENDANGER LIFE IN ANYWAY. IT IS ALSO A MESSAGE BY
GOD, TO YOU, TO REMIND YOU OF THE POWER YOU

HOLD IN CREATING THE EXPERIENCES FOR YOURSELF BY KNOWING "WHO YOU REALLY ARE."

THIS IS BEAUTIFUL, THIS IS POWER AND I AM BASKING IN THE LIGHT OF THIS KNOWLEDGE THAT HAS BEEN GIVEN UNTO ME, THROUGH ME, TO YOU. I AM VERY HAPPY AND EXCITED IN BEING ABLE AND WILLING TO SHARE THIS WITH YOU, FOR NOW IT IS MINE TO GIVE, AND WHAT I GIVE TO YOU THIS DAY, I GIVE TO MYSELF. LET US REJOICE TOGETHER IN LOVE, IN PEACE, IN HARMONY, IN JOY, IN CONTENTMENT, AND IN HAPPINESS THIS VERY DAY FOR HAVING FOUND THIS REBORN LIGHT FOREVER. I PRAY AND I WILL THAT YOU SEE THIS IN A MOST WONDROUS WAY. DO YOU HAVE ANY QUESTIONS? YES YOU DO AND THIS IS WHAT WE ARE SEEING NEXT.

QUESTION

LET US NOW LOOK UPON THE WORD "QUESTION". WHAT DOES IT DEFINE? IS IT THE ASKING FOR AN ANSWER TO WHAT YOU WISH TO KNOW? OF COURSE IT IS. LET'S DIVIDE THIS WORD UP IN PIECES.

"QUEST"

"I"

"ON"

SO WHEN YOU SAY,

"I HAVE A QUESTION",

YOU ARE SAYING,

"I HAVE A QUEST {JOURNEY} I AM ON",

IN OTHER WORDS

"I SEEK KNOWLEDGE BY WAY OF AN ANSWER, TO CONTINUE THE JOURNEY I AM ON".

WORDS LIKE THIS ARE SOMETHING TO BE AWARE OF. I CAN SAFELY COME TO A DEFINING MOMENT, THAT THE NEXT TIME YOU ASK A QUESTION, THAT YOU WILL SEE IT IN A DIFFERENT LIGHT, FOR NOW, THE WAY YOU SEE THIS, YOU WILL ASK YOURSELF,

"WHAT IS THE QUEST THAT I AM ON THAT HAD ME ASK THE QUESTION IN THE FIRST PLACE?"

THIS WILL GIVE YOU AN INNER LIGHT AS TO WHAT YOUR SOUL IS WISHING TO EXPERIENCE, WHICH IN TURN WILL MAKE YOUR SOUL KNOWN TO YOU, BECOMING CONSCIOUS OF YOUR UNCONSCIOUS, AND THEREFOR BECOMING "ONE WITH GOD!", THAT IS A VERY SPECIAL QUEST, A FANTASTIC SPIRITUAL JOURNEY!

I AWOKE ONE MORNING AT 3:30 A.M. WITH THIS CONSTANT PHRASE GOING THROUGH MY MIND. I HAD TO GET UP AND WRITE IT DOWN, AS I WROTE THE PHRASE DOWN A FEW MORE CAME IN THE SAME PHRASE BUT DIFFERENT VERSIONS. THEY ARE AS FOLLOWS.

1. "YOUR QUESTION IS ALWAYS IN THE ASKING OF YOUR ANSWER."

2. "YOUR QUESTION IS ALWAYS IN THE ANSWER YOU ARE ASKING."

3. "YOUR ANSWER IS ALWAYS IN THE ASKING OF YOUR QUESTION."

4. "YOUR ANSWER IS ALWAYS IN THE QUESTION YOU ARE ASKING."

HAVING CONTEMPLATED ON THESE PHRASES, THE LIGHT HAS PRESENTED ITSELF.

1. "YOUR QUESTION IS ALWAYS IN THE ASKING OF YOUR ANSWER."

1. "YOU R, QUEST {JOURNEY} I ON, IS ALL WAYS, IN THEE, AS KING {POWER} OF,   YOU R ANSWER {KNOWLEDGE}.

IN OTHER WORDS,

1. "YOU ARE, THE JOURNEY I AM ON, IS IN ALL WAYS, IN THEE, AS THE POWER OF, YOU ARE KNOWLEDGE."

2. "YOUR QUESTION IS ALWAYS IN THE ANSWER YOU ARE ASKING".

2. "YOU R, THE QUEST {JOURNEY} I ON, IS ALWAYS, IN THE ANSWER   {KNOWLEDGE}, YOU R, AS KING {POWER}.

IN OTHER WORDS,

2. "YOU ARE, THE JOURNEY I AM ON, IS IN ALL WAYS, IN THE KNOWLEDGE, YOU   ARE, AS POWER."

3. "YOUR ANSWER IS ALWAYS IN THE ASKING OF YOUR QUESTION."

3. "YOU R, ANSWER {KNOWLEDGE}, IS ALL WAYS, IN THEE, AS KING {POWER} OF,   YOU R QUEST {JOURNEY}, I ON."

IN OTHER WORDS,

3. "YOU ARE KNOWLEDGE, IS ALL WAYS IN THEE, AS THE POWER OF, YOU ARE   THE JOURNEY I AM ON."

4. "YOUR ANSWER IS ALWAYS IN THE QUESTION YOU ARE ASKING."

4. "YOU R, ANSWER {KNOWLEDGE} IS ALL WAYS, IN THE QUEST {JOURNEY} I ON, YOU R AS KING {POWER}."

IN OTHER WORDS,

4. "YOU ARE KNOWLEDGE, IS ALL WAYS, IN THEE, JOURNEY I AM ON, YOU ARE AS POWER."

THIS IS TRULY AMAZING INFORMATION. IT IS A MESSAGE TO ME, THROUGH ME, TO GIVE TO YOU.

"YOU ARE THE KING, YOU ARE THE POWER AND THE QUEST YOU ARE ON, THE JOURNEY YOU ARE ON, IS TO KNOW "WHO YOU REALLY ARE", AND THAT IS "PURE POSITIVE ENERGY", " A HIGHLY POWERFUL, HIGHLY POSITIVE SPIRITUAL BEING", AND THAT IS "ONENESS WITH GOD", BRING THE HOLY TRINITY OF YOUR THOUGHTS, YOUR WORDS {SPEECH}, AND YOUR EXPERIENCE/ACTIONS TOGETHER AS "ONE", INTO CONSCIOUSNESS/KNOWINGNESS, AND NOW THAT YOU KNOW THIS, WE WILL TOGETHER CREATE "HEAVEN ON EARTH",

"PURE POSITIVE ENERGY"

THAT IS

"ALL LOVING",

"ALL CARING",

"ALL KNOWING",

"ALL GIVING",
"ALL HAPPINESS",

AND

"ALL POWERFUL",

CREATED HERE ON EARTH, MANIFESTED INTO PHYSICAL FORM SO THAT WE WILL

"LIVE IT"

AND THAT DEFINES AS

"WE WILL EXPERIENCE"

THIS LOVE, THIS JOY FOREVER IN PHYSICAL FORM. THIS BRINGS JOY INTO MY BEING AND I SEE NOW, AS YOU DO ALSO, THE GOAL

"ALL OF US"

HAVE SET FOR OURSELVES, BEFORE BIRTH, THE REALIZATION THAT WE HAVE REACHED THIS GOAL OF PRESENTING "HEAVEN ON EARTH", IS NOW HERE.
    NOW, THE NEXT TIME SOMEONE ASKS YOU A QUESTION AND IF YOU HAVE THE ANSWER THEN HELP THEM WITH THE QUEST THEY ARE ON FOR IT WILL HELP YOU WITH THE JOURNEY YOU ARE ON, FOR WHEN YOU DO THIS, THE LIGHT WILL SHINE UPON YOU BRIGHTLY

AND YOUR SOUL WILL BASK IN THE LIGHT MAKING ITSELF BE KNOWN TO YOU. YOU WILL SEE FOR YOURSELF.

"YOU"

"R"
"SELF."

THIS IS AWESOME, IS IT NOT? THE ANSWER IS NO, IT IS NOT AWESOME, WHAT IT IS, IS BEAUTIFUL IN KNOWING. AWESOME, BY DEFINITION IS, AN EMOTION VARIOUSLY COMBINING DREAD, VENERATION, AND WONDER THAT IS INSPIRED BY AUTHORITY OR BY THE SACRED OR SUBLIME. AS IN, {STOOD IN AWE OF THE KING} {STOOD IN AWE OF THE POWER YOU HOLD}. YOU WILL NOT STAND IN DREAD OR WONDERMENT OF THE POWER YOU POSSESS. YOU WILL STAND IN THE LIGHT OF BEAUTY, THE LIGHT OF KNOWING HOW POWERFUL YOU TRULY ARE BY CREATING YOUR WORLD CONSCIOUSLY. THIS IS THE WHOLE POINT OF THIS BOOK, TO SHOW YOU HOW POWERFUL YOU ARE TO CREATE A WORLD OF BEAUTY AND OF LOVE!

CREATION, AGAIN

CREATION COMES TO YOU AT THE SPEED OF LIGHT, WHICH IS 186,000 MILES PER SECOND, NOW YOU CAN TEST THIS OUT. WHENEVER YOU HAVE RUBBED YOUR EYES, WHEN THEY ARE CLOSED, WHAT DO YOU REMEMBER SEEING?

"IT IS LITTLE SPECKS OF LIGHT",

SOMETIMES THEY ARE DIFFERENT COLORS AND SOMETIMES THEY ARE WHITE, ALL DIFFERENT SHAPES AND SIZES AND THE MOMENT YOU OPEN YOUR EYES, WHAT DO YOU SEE NEXT?

"IT IS DARKNESS",

THEN EVERYTHING STARTS TO COME INTO FOCUS LIKE A DOT MATRIX. THIS IS YOUR CREATION MANIFESTING RIGHT IN FRONT OF YOU. IT IS YOUR THOUGHTS, YOUR WORDS {SPEECH}, AND YOUR EXPERIENCE/ACTION THAT YOU HAVE CREATED TO COMPARE YOURSELF TO.

"THE QUESTION IS",

"WHAT BROUGHT YOU TO RUB YOUR EYES IN THE FIRST PLACE?"

"IS IT TO REFOCUS ON A LIFE, THAT YOU HAVE CREATED, THAT NO LONGER SERVES YOU?"

BY THAT, I WILL DEFINE IT AS

"SOMETHING YOU WISH TO BE MORE POSITIVE ABOUT".

WHEN YOU RUB YOUR EYES, IT IS YOUR SOUL, REMINDING YOU, THAT YOU WILL CREATE A MORE RELAXING, MORE POSITIVE LIFE. YOUR SOUL IS REMINDING YOU THAT,

"YOU ARE THE POWER THAT RECREATES YOUR LIFE",

BY SHOWING YOU HOW YOUR CREATION IS COMING AT YOU,

"BY THE SPEED OF LIGHT".

AFTER RUBBING YOUR EYES, HAVE YOU EVER NOTICED WHAT YOUR REACTION IS TO THAT?

"YOU IMMEDIATELY, GO INTO A CALMING, MEDITATIVE STATE."

"THIS IS YOUR BODY REACTING TO THE RELAXATION OF KNOWING!"

NOW THAT YOU KNOW THE "WHY", THE REASON FOR RUBBING YOUR EYES, AS A REMINDER THAT YOU CAN CHANGE THE SITUATION YOU ARE IN, LET'S GET INTO THE "HOW" DO WE CHANGE THE SITUATION TO A MORE POSITIVE STATE?

HOW DO WE CHANGE OVER TO POSITIVITY

KNOWING, NOW, THAT CREATION BEGINS WITH OUR POSITIVE THOUGHTS, COMBINED WITH OUR POSITIVE WORDS OF SPEECH, THAT GIVES TO US OUR EXPERIENCE TO PRODUCE OUR ACTIONS OF OUR CREATION, WHICH IS THE

"QUESTION",

"THE JOURNEY WE ARE ON",

WE WILL NOW COMBINE OUR TOTAL KNOWLEDGE TO CREATE CONSCIOUSLY OUR DESIRE INTO MANIFESTATION.

KNOWING THAT

"THE LORD'S PRAYER",

IS A

"COMMAND PRAYER",
A

"PROTECTION PRAYER",

AND A

"MESSAGE PRAYER",

THAT PUTS FORTH THE ENERGY TO BRING OUR
THOUGHTS, OUR SPEECH, AND OUR EXPERIENCE INTO
MANIFESTATION ON THE EARTHLY PLANE. WE WILL
UTILIZE THIS PRAYER AFTER STATING WHAT OUR
CREATION IS TO BE ABOUT. IT IS BEST TO BE STANDING
WITH YOUR HANDS IN THE AIR.
   BIO ENERGY, LIFE ENERGY, COMES INTO THE BODY
ON THE LEFT SIDE OF THE BODY,

"THIS IS ENERGY THAT YOU RECEIVE, THIS IS THE
ENERGY OF YOUR ENVIRONMENT AND THE THOUGHTS
OF OTHERS."

"THE CHAKRAS",

IN THE MIDDLE OF THE BODY,

"DETERMINE WHERE THAT ENERGY IS BEST SUITED FOR
YOUR BODY AND PLACES THAT ENERGY IN YOUR BODY",

"THEN YOUR THOUGHTS AND IMPRESSIONS EXIT

THROUGH THE RIGHT SIDE OF YOUR BODY".

WHEN YOU ARE LISTENING TO SOMEONE SPEAK, AND IF
YOU ARE INTERESTED IN WHAT THEY HAVE TO SAY,
THEN TURN YOUR LEFT SIDE TOWARD THEM, THIS WILL
ENABLE YOU TO EASILY KNOW THE MESSAGE THEY ARE
SAYING TO YOU AND MOST TIMES YOU WILL KNOW
WHAT THEY ARE ABOUT TO SAY BEFORE THEY EVEN
SAY IT. IF YOU ARE SPEAKING AND WISH TO GET YOUR
MESSAGE KNOWN TO THE PEOPLE YOU ARE TALKING
TO, THEN TURN YOUR RIGHT SIDE TOWARD THEM. THEY
WILL RECEIVE YOUR MESSAGE MUCH MORE CLEARER
AND YOU WILL GAIN MORE ATTENTION FROM THEM.

"THIS IS WHY IT IS IMPORTANT TO HAVE YOUR ARMS
AND HANDS RAISED WHEN IN PRAYER/CREATING".

THE FOLLOWING IS A SAMPLE PRAYER. START OUT
WITH,

"I COMMAND THEE",

"IN THE NAME OF, {BY AUTHORITY OF} THE FATHER, THE
SON, AND THE HOLY SPIRIT".

THEN STATE WHAT YOU ARE WISHING TO CREATE AND
BE SPECIFIC IN YOUR ASKING,

"TO GIVE TO ME THE "PURE POSITIVE ENERGY", OF
THAT WHICH I ALREADY AM IN HEAVEN FORM, TO MAKE
PRESENT AND TO MANIFEST WITHIN ME IN EARTHLY
FORM. GIVE TO ME THE LOVE, THE PEACE, THE JOY, THE
HAPPINESS, OF WHICH I ALREADY AM, INTO MY MORTAL
LIFE, SO THAT I WILL APPRECIATE MY HUMAN BEING
INTO POSITIVITY".

THEN FOLLOW UP WITH "THE LORD'S PRAYER."

OUR FATHER, WHO ART IN HEAVEN
HALLOWED BE THY NAME
THY KINGDOM COME
THY WILL BE DONE
ON EARTH AS IT IS IN HEAVEN
GIVE US THIS DAY OUR DAILY BREAD
AND FORGIVE US OUR TRESPASSES
AS WE FORGIVE THOSE WHO HAVE TRESPASSED
AGAINST US
AND LEAD US NOT INTO TEMPTATION
BUT DELIVER US FROM EVIL
FOR THINE IS THE POWER AND THE GLORY IN THE
KINGDOM
FOREVER AND EVER
AMEN!

GIVE ATTENTION TO HOW THIS PRAYER IS SET UP. IT IS IN THREE PARTS.

"I COMMAND THEE" OR "I WILL THEE"

IS PLACING THE ENERGY INTO MOTION, REMEMBER THAT WORD "WILL" PLACES INTO MOTION THE ENERGY {EMOTION} TO MAKE MANIFEST YOUR CREATION.

"COMMAND" IS "WILL"

"COMMAND" IS "I COMMUNICATE MY MANNED THOUGHT OF ME".

"IN THE NAME OF" IS DEFINING "BY AUTHORITY OF".

YOU ARE COMMANDING/WILLING YOUR SOUL TO BE AWARE OF THE CREATION YOU ARE MAKING.

WHEN YOU SAY

"IN THE NAME OF",

YOU ARE LETTING YOUR SOUL BE AWARE OF WHERE
THIS CREATION IS COMING FROM,
"BY THE AUTHORITY {AUTHOR} OF,

"THE FATHER, YOUR THOUGHTS",

"THE SON, YOUR WORDS",

AND

"THE HOLY SPIRIT, YOUR EXPERIENCE/ACTION".

THIS ALLOWS THE SOUL TO KNOW YOU HAVE COMBINED
THOSE THREE "THE HOLY TRINITY" INTO "ONE" BEING,
READY FOR MANIFESTATION.

    THE SECOND PORTION IS LETTING YOUR SOUL KNOW,
WHAT IT IS, THAT YOU ARE WISHING TO CREATE, THIS IS
WHERE YOUR SPEECH AND THE WORDS THAT YOU USE
ARE VERY IMPORTANT, BECAUSE YOU WILL RECEIVE
EXACTLY WHAT YOU ARE SAYING YOU ARE DESIRING TO
EXPERIENCE.
    THE THIRD PORTION, BEING "THE LORD'S PRAYER",
PLACES YOUR ENERGY INTO MANIFESTATION SAFELY. IT

"WILLS"

YOUR ENERGY,

"YOUR SOUL",

IT PROTECTS

"YOUR LIFE"

AND THE

"LIFE OF OTHERS",
AND IT REMINDS YOUR SOUL THAT IT IS WRAPPED
AROUND YOUR BODY AND THAT IT HAS THE POWER TO
CREATE YOUR MANIFESTATION OF EXPERIENCE.
    YES, THIS IS VERY POWERFUL INFORMATION TO
KNOW AND TO REMIND YOU TO KNOW THAT,

"WHAT YOU SAY OF OTHERS, YOU ARE SAYING ABOUT
YOURSELF AND WHAT YOU WISH TO EXPERIENCE".

SO,

"WHAT YOU ASK OF OTHERS IN YOUR PRAYERS IS WHAT
YOU ASK OF YOURSELF",

"WHAT YOU GIVE TO OTHERS IN YOUR PRAYERS, YOU
ARE GIVING TO YOURSELF".

THEREFORE, GO AND SEEK FOR YOURSELF ONLY
POSITIVITY AND

"FOR GIVE"

WITH YOUR ENERGY ALL POSITIVITY FOR YOU AND ALL
THAT ENTER INTO YOUR LIFE!

HEALING

HEALING IS VERY MUCH A PART OF OUR EARTHLY LIFE. IT IS A NECESSARY PART OF MORTAL LIFE, FOR WHEN WE CREATE OUR MORTAL LIFE SUBCONSCIOUSLY, WE REACT TO OUR CREATIONS, AND KNOWING NOW, HOW THE AGING PROCESS IS SELF INFLICTED UPON US BY REACTING TO LIFE, WE WILL NOW HEAL OUR BODY, WITH THE KNOWLEDGE OF KNOWING HOW TO CONSCIOUSLY CREATE THE HEALING ENERGY OF POSITIVITY AND FOREVER KEEP THE POSITIVE ENERGY FLOWING TO US AND THEN THROUGH US.

"WHAT GOT US HERE, TO THIS POINT OF HEALING, OUR BODIES, IN THE FIRST PLACE?"

THAT IS A SIMPLE ANSWER AND IF YOU HAVEN'T REMEMBERED IT YET, THEN HERE IT IS AGAIN.

"AS SOUL ENERGY,"

"WE ARE PURE POSITIVE ENERGY",

"NO MANIFESTED PHYSICAL BEING",

"THE ALL KNOWING, THE ALL POWERFUL, THE ALL LOVING"

AND WE EXIST, IN THIS STATE OF BEING, WITH A DESIRE OF KNOWING

"WHAT AND WHO WE REALLY ARE."

THE ONLY WAY WE CAN DO THIS IS TO CREATE OUR PHYSICAL BEING,

"MORTAL LIFE",

SO THAT WE MAY FEEL

"WHAT AND WHO WE REALLY ARE",

AND TO CREATE

"THE OPPOSITE OF WHAT AND WHO WE REALLY ARE",
BY CREATING NEGATIVITY. THIS PROVES TO OUR SOUL
THAT

"WE ARE PURE POSITIVE ENERGY",

THOUGH YOUR MORTAL EARTHLY MIND, DOES NOT
THINK SO

YOUR HEAVENLY SOUL NOW KNOWS.

"IT DOES NOT MATTER", WHAT YOUR SOUL DOES TO
YOUR EARTHLY BODY, AS LONG AS IT IS REMINDED OF
IT'S BEING AS "PURE POSITIVE ENERGY", BECAUSE YOUR
SOUL KNOWS IT CAN AND WILL CREATE ANOTHER
EARTHLY BODY TO CONTINUE IT TO RE-MEMBER ITSELF.
THIS IS WHY YOU HAVE MANY LIFETIMES TO ACHIEVE

"ENLIGHTENMENT".

WHEN YOU HAVE ARRIVED AT THIS POINT, AND YOU
NOW HAVE, IT IS NOW UP TO YOU, WHAT YOU WISH TO
BE.

"YOU HAVE COME THIS FAR."

"WILL YOU GO FURTHER?"

AFTER READING WHAT YOU HAVE, YOU KNOW YOU
POSSESS THE POWER TO HAVE ANYTHING AND

EVERYTHING YOU DESIRE AND WISH FOR.

"IT IS YOUR DECISION TO FULLY APPLY THIS KNOWLEDGE, THE INTELLIGENCE {APPLICATION} OF PLACING INTO MOTION YOUR CONSCIOUS/KNOWING BEING".

"YOU ARE NOW CONSCIOUS OF WHO YOU REALLY ARE."

THE POWER YOU POSSESS WILL NOW HEAL YOUR BODY INTO IMMORTALITY IF YOU SO DESIRE THIS TO BE.

"THE POWER OF YOUR HEALING IS IN THE POWER OF YOUR PRAYERS."

RETURNING THE BODY BACK TO FULL EFFICIENT ENERGY OF YOUTH. THE FOLLOWING IS A SAMPLE PRAYER THAT YOU MAY USE.

STAND FACING TO THE SOUTH AND WITH YOUR LEFT HAND RAISED TO THE EAST AND YOUR RIGHT HAND OVER YOUR LIVER. THE LIVER IS THE MOST IMPORTANT ORGAN OF YOUR BODY, IT CONTROLS ALL OTHER ORGANS, IT IS LOCATED ON YOUR RIGHT SIDE UNDER YOUR RIB CAGE AND EXTENDS UPWARDS TOWARD THE HEART.

NOTE NOW, THINK OF WHY IT IS CALLED THE LIVER {LIVE}!

YOU CAN PLACE YOUR RIGHT HAND OVER ANY PART OF THE BODY, REMEMBER THE LEFT SIDE IS THE INTAKE OF ENERGY, THE RIGHT SIDE IS THE OUTGOING OF YOUR ENERGY.

NOW SAY,

"I COMMAND THEE"

"IN THE NAME OF THE FATHER, THE SON, AND THE HOLY SPIRIT",

"TO HEAL THIS BODY AND IT'S ORGANS SO THAT THIS BODY WILL RETURN TO FULL ENERGETIC HEALTH, GIVE TO THIS BODY, WHICH I AM WRAPPED AROUND, ALL PURE POSITIVE ENERGY, ALL LOVE, ALL HAPPINESS, ALL PEACE, AND ALL PROSPERITY FOR WHAT IT TRULY IS, SO THAT I WILL FULLY APPRECIATE LIFE ON EARTH, IN SO BEING, I WILL CREATE HEAVEN ON EARTH"!

THEN FOLLOW UP WITH "THE LORD'S PRAYER."

"OUR FATHER, WHO ART IN HEAVEN
HALLOWED BE THY NAME
THY KINGDOM COME
THY WILL BE DONE
ON EARTH AS IT IS IN HEAVEN
GIVE US THIS DAY OUR DAILY BREAD
AND FORGIVE US OUR TRESPASSES
  AS WE FORGIVE THOSE WHO HAVE TRESPASSED
AGAINST US
AND LEAD US NOT INTO TEMPTATION
BUT DELIVER US FROM EVIL
FOR THINE IS THE POWER AND THE GLORY IN THE KINGDOM
FOREVER AND EVER
AMEN"!

NOW STILL FACING TO THE SOUTH, BRING YOUR LEFT HAND OVER TO YOUR LIVER AND YOUR RIGHT HAND RAISED TO THE WEST AND SAY THE FOLLOWING,

"I COMMAND THEE",

"IN THE NAME OF THE FATHER, THE SON, AND THE HOLY SPIRIT",

"TO HEAL THIS BODY BY RELEASING ALL NEGATIVITY FROM MY BODY AND FROM MY THOUGHTS. I AM THANKFUL FOR THE EXPERIENCE YOU HAVE GIVEN UNTO ME AND IN THAT YOU NO LONGER SERVE ME, ANY NEGATIVITY WITHIN MY BODY AND WITHIN MY THOUGHTS WILL LEAVE ME AND GO BACK INTO THE UNIVERSE WITH MY LOVE AND GOD'S BLESSING SO THAT I WILL CREATE HEAVEN ON EARTH"!

THEN FOLLOW UP WITH "THE LORD'S PRAYER",

"OUR FATHER, WHO ART IN HEAVEN
HALLOWED BE THY NAME
THY KINGDOM COME
THY WILL BE DONE
ON EARTH AS IT IS IN HEAVEN
GIVE US THIS DAY OUR DAILY BREAD
AND FORGIVE US OUR TRESPASSES
AS WE FORGIVE THOSE WHO HAVE TRESPASSED
AGAINST US
AND LEAD US NOT INTO TEMPTATION
BUT DELIVER US FROM EVIL
FOR THINE IS THE POWER AND THE GLORY IN THE KINGDOM
FOREVER AND EVER
AMEN"!

IF YOU ARE HEALING SOMEONE ELSE, AND REMEMBER THIS,

"IF YOU DECLARE YOURSELF TO BE A HEALER, THEN

YOU CREATE THOSE THAT MUST BE HEALED",

IT IS,

IN ALL ESSENCE,

"YOUR CREATION",
AND THEY HAVE COME TO YOU FOR HEALING.

WITH BOTH OF YOU FACING SOUTH, YOU PLACE YOUR LEFT HAND IN THE AIR TOWARD THE EAST,

NOTE THE SUN RISES IN THE EAST, BRINGING A FRESH NEW DAY, THE SUN SETS IN THE WEST, RETIRING THE DAY.

WITH YOUR RIGHT HAND, GRAB AND HOLD THEIR LEFT HAND, HAVE THEM PLACE THEIR RIGHT HAND ON TO THEIR LIVER , PALM DOWN, THEN YOU SAY THIS,

"I COMMAND THEE",

"IN THE NAME OF THE FATHER, THE SON, AND THE HOLY SPIRIT",

"THAT THROUGH ME, YOU WILL HEAL THIS BODY AND IT'S ORGANS OF <u>FULL NAME OF THE PERSON YOU ARE HEALING</u>, IN WHICH THEY ARE WRAPPED AROUND, SO THAT IT WILL RETURN TO FULL ENERGETIC HEALTH. GIVE TO THIS BODY OF <u>FULL NAME OF THE PERSON YOU ARE HEALING</u>, THE LIGHT OF ENERGY OF KNOWING WHO THEY REALLY ARE, ALL PURE POSITIVE ENERGY, ALL LOVE, ALL PEACE, ALL HAPPINESS, AND ALL PROSPERITY, FOR WHAT IT TRULY IS, SO THAT THEY WILL FULLY APPRECIATE LIFE ON EARTH AND IN SO BEING, WE WILL TOGETHER CREATE HEAVEN ON

EARTH"!

FOLLOW UP WITH "THE LORD'S PRAYER",

"OUR FATHER, WHO ART IN HEAVEN
HALLOWED BE THY NAME
THY KINGDOM COME
THY WILL BE DONE
ON EARTH AS IT IS IN HEAVEN
GIVE US THIS DAY OUR DAILY BREAD
AND FORGIVE US OUR TRESPASSES
AS WE FORGIVE THOSE WHO HAVE TRESPASSED
AGAINST US
AND LEAD US NOT INTO TEMPTATION
BUT DELIVER US FROM EVIL
FOR THINE IS THE POWER AND THE GLORY IN THE
KINGDOM
FOREVER AND EVER
AMEN"!

AS YOU RELEASE YOUR HANDS FROM EACH OTHER,
MOVE TO THE BACK OF THEM, THIS WILL BE TO THE
NORTH AND COME OVER TO THEIR RIGHT SIDE, WEST
SIDE. HAVE THEM PLACE THEIR LEFT HAND OVER THEIR
LIVER AND YOU TAKE YOUR LEFT HAND, GRAB AND
HOLD THEIR RIGHT HAND, THEN RAISE YOUR RIGHT
HAND TO THE WEST WITH YOUR PALM UP TO ALLOW
EXIT OF ENERGY THROUGH YOU. NOW SAY THIS,

"I COMMAND THEE",

"IN THE NAME OF THE FATHER, THE SON, AND THE HOLY
SPIRIT",

"THAT THROUGH ME, YOU WILL HEAL THIS BODY AND
IT'S ORGANS OF <u>FULL NAME OF THE PERSON BEING</u>

147

HEALED, OF WHICH THEY ARE WRAPPED AROUND, BY RELEASING ALL NEGATIVITY OF THIS MIND AND THIS BODY. FULL NAME OF THE PERSON BEING HEALED, AND I ARE THANKFUL FOR THE EXPERIENCE YOU HAVE GIVEN UNTO THEM AND IN THAT YOU NO LONGER SERVE THEM. ANY NEGATIVITY IN THIS BODY AND IN THEIR MIND WILL NOW LEAVE THEM, THROUGH ME, AND WILL GO BACK INTO THE UNIVERSE WITH OUR LOVE AND GOD'S BLESSING AND IN SO DOING WE WILL TOGETHER CREATE HEAVEN ON EARTH"!

THEN FOLLOW UP WITH "THE LORD'S PRAYER",

"OUR FATHER, WHO ART IN HEAVEN
HALLOWED BE THY NAME
THY KINGDOM COME
THY WILL BE DONE
ON EARTH AS IT IS IN HEAVEN
GIVE US THIS DAY OUR DAILY BREAD
AND FORGIVE US OUR TRESPASSES
AS WE FORGIVE THOSE WHO HAVE TRESPASSED
AGAINST US
AND LEAD US NOT INTO TEMPTATION
BUT DELIVER US FROM EVIL
FOR THINE IS THE POWER AND THE GLORY IN THE
KINGDOM
FOREVER AND EVER
AMEN"!

OVER THE HILL

NOW WITH ALL OF THIS KNOWLEDGE YOU HAVE OBTAINED THIS FAR, YOU NOW HOLD THE POWER OF YOUR LIFE AND YOUR WORLD AT YOUR BECKONED

CALL.

"WHAT WILL YOU DO WITH THIS?"

"WHAT WILL YOU BECOME OF THIS?"

IT IS YOUR WORLD AND I APPRECIATE YOU ALLOWING ME TO BE A PART OF IT.

   REMEMBER THIS, IF YOU LIVE IN NEED OR WANT THEN YOU LIVE IN DESPERATION, THEN YOU LIVE IN

"DE" = "OF" OR "OF THE"

"SPERATION" = A POINT, LINE, OR MEANS OF DIVISION. AN INTERVENING SPACE.   TO SET OR KEEP APART".

SEPARATION OF THE "HOLY TRINITY",

"THE FATHER, YOUR THOUGHTS",

"THE SON, YOUR WORDS",

"THE HOLY SPIRIT, YOUR SOUL/EXPERIENCE/ACTION",

AND YOU RECEIVE EXACTLY THAT.

WHEN YOU LIVE YOUR LIFE WITH

"IMAGINATION",

AND WHAT DOES "IMAGINATION" DEFINE?

"I" = "SOMEONE AWARE OF POSSESSING A PERSONAL INDIVIDUALITY."

"MAGI" = "A MEMBER OF AN HEREDITARY PRIESTLY CLASS AMONG THE   ANCIENTS. SPIRITUAL POWER!"

"NATION" = "TO BE BORN",

IN OTHER WORDS THAT ARE DEFINING "IMAGINATION",

"I AM THE SPIRITUAL POWER TO BE BORN"!

POSITIVE IMAGINATION WILL GIVE TO YOU POSITIVE SPIRITUAL POWER FOR A HAPPY LIFE. SO THAT YOU CAN

"DEFINE"

"YOU".

WHAT IS THE DEFINITION OF "DEFINE"?

"DE" = "OF" OR "OF THE"

"FINE" = "FREE FROM IMPURITY, VERY PRECISE OR ACCURATE".

SO WHEN WE "DEFINE" WHO WE REALLY ARE,

"WE ARE BEING FREE FROM IMPURITY, VERY PRECISE AND ACCURATE, AND THAT IS "PURE POSITIVE ENERGY".

   YOU ARE NOW, "OVER THE HILL". MOSTLY THIS TERM IS USED TO EXPRESS SOMEONE THAT HAS REACHED A CERTAIN AGE, DEFINING MATURITY, IN ALL ACTUALITY IT IS DEFINING AS,

"HAVING ENOUGH EXPERIENCES OF NEGATIVITY TO

FULLY KNOW "YOU ARE PURE POSITIVE ENERGY", AND
WILL CREATE YOUR WORLD KNOWINGLY THROUGH

"YOUR POSITIVE THOUGHTS",

"YOUR POSITIVE WORDS",

AND

"YOUR POSITIVE ACTIONS OF EXPERIENCE".

THEREFOR, WITH THE KNOWLEDGE YOU HAVE
REMEMBERED,

"YOU ARE NOW",

"OVER THE HILL",

FOR THE HILLS THAT YOU HAVE DREADED ARE NOW
REMOVED BY THE HUGE STEP YOU HAVE TAKEN, WILL
NOW, BY THE POWER YOU CONSCIOUSLY POSSESS, TO
CREATE GREENER PASTURES IN A FIELD FULL OF
ABUNDANCE AND FERTILITY.

"YOU ARE THE BEING THAT HOLDS THE LIGHT OF THE
FUTURE",

"YOU ARE THE FUTURE OF THE LIGHT INTO BEING".

I GIVE TO YOU THIS POEM THAT IS DEFINING TO US ALL.

WHAT WILL YOU DO WHEN YOUR KNOWLEDGE UNFOLDS
WHAT WILL YOU BE WHEN YOUR STORY IS TOLD
WHAT WILL YOU SEEK WHEN THE DARK TURNS TO
LIGHT
WHAT WILL YOU SEE AS THE LIGHT SHINES SO BRIGHT

THESE QUESTIONS I ASK ARE THE FUTURE YOU HOLD
OF LIFE EVERLASTING, OF YOUTH NEVER OLD
LOVE YOURSELF ALWAYS AND GIVE OF THE SAME
FOR WHAT YOU DO GIVE IT RETURNS TO REMAIN
SO GIVE OF YOUR LOVE AND THIS KNOWLEDGE NOT
SMALL
FOR THE POWER YOU HOLD IS THE POWER OF ALL!
I AM ASKING FOR YOU TO NOW JOIN ME IN PRAYER AS
WE COME TO THE END OF THIS BOOK THAT GIVES TO US
A NEW BEGINNING OF A NEW LIFE. ONE OF STRENGTH
AND COURAGE, LOVE AND POWER, COMPASSION AND
FOR GIVING OF OUR NEW POSITIVE ENERGY THAT IS
NOW FOREVER FLOWING. STAND FACING TO THE SOUTH
AND RAISE YOUR HANDS, LEFT TO THE EAST AND RIGHT
TO THE WEST, OBSERVE THE ENERGY FLOW INTO YOUR
BODY AND THEN THROUGH YOUR BODY AND THE
PULSATING OF YOUR RIGHT HAND AS IT EXITS YOUR
BODY.

"I COMMAND THEE",

"IN THE NAME OF THE FATHER, THE SON, AND THE HOLY
SPIRIT",

" TO APPRECIATE THIS KNOWLEDGE INTO MY LIFE, THE
LIGHT HAS SHINED UPON ME BRIGHTLY AND WITH THE
POWER THAT I NOW KNOW I POSSESS WILL CREATE ALL
POSITIVITY IN MY LIFE AND MY WORLD, WE ARE
THANKFUL OF THE NEGATIVITY THAT HAS BEEN
PRESENTED TO US, THROUGH THIS BOOK AND THROUGH
OUT OUR LIFE, FOR WE NOW KNOW THAT WE HAVE
CREATED SUCH AN ENTITY AND THAT WE CLAIM
OWNERSHIP OF THIS CREATION AND SEEING THAT IT
HAS SERVED IT'S PURPOSE WELL IN KNOWING HOW
POWERFUL WE ARE TO CREATE THIS ENTITY, WE
RELEASE ANY AND ALL NEGATIVITY BACK INTO THE

UNIVERSE WITH OUR LOVE AND GOD'S BLESSING SO
THAT OUR FUTURE WILL BUILD ONLY UPON PURE
POSITIVITY, WHICH IS LOVE, TO APPRECIATE THIS INTO
OUR CREATION OF HEAVEN ON EARTH!

"OUR FATHER, WHO ART IN HEAVEN
HALLOWED BE THY NAME
THY KINGDOM COME
THY WILL BE DONE
ON EARTH AS IT IS IN HEAVEN
GIVE US THIS DAY OUR DAILY BREAD
AND FORGIVE US OUR TRESPASSES
AS WE FORGIVE THOSE WHO HAVE TRESPASSED
AGAINST US
AND LEAD US NOT INTO TEMPTATION
BUT DELIVER US FROM EVIL
FOR THINE IS THE POWER AND THE GLORY IN THE
KINGDOM
FOREVER AND EVER
AMEN"!

   I GIVE TO YOU MY LOVE, FOR THIS IS WHAT IS
DEFINING,

"WHO I REALLY AM"!

"MAY GOD ALWAYS BE WITH YOU",

"AS GOD ALWAYS IS",

"MAY YOU BE WITH GOD",

"AS YOU ALWAYS ARE"!

WITH LOVE AND AFFECTION IN ALL WAYS

"A SPIRIT OF GOD"

ANY QUESTIONS, COMMENTS, OR CONCERNS CAN BE EMAILED TO

deepeagle@hotmail.com

ADDRESS THE SUBJECT MATTER AS

"THE HILLS".

THE AUTHOR